ILLUSTRATED DICTIONARY OF CARGO HANDLING
FOURTH EDITION

BY PETER BRODIE

Illustrated Dictionary of Cargo Handling, 4th Edition (2015)
Dictionary of Shipping Terms, 6th Edition (2013)
Illustrated Dictionary of Cargo Handling, 3rd Edition (2010)
Commercial Shipping Handbook, 3rd Edition (2015)

RELATED TITLES

Introduction to Marine Cargo Management, Second Edition, 2014
Freight Forwarding and Multi-Modal Transport, Second Edition, David Glass, 2012
The Handbook of Maritime Economic and Business, Costas Th. Grammenos, 2010
Port Operations and Risk Management, Khalid Bichou, 2009
Risk Management in Port Operations, Logistics and Supply Chain Security, Khalid Bichou, Mike Bell and Andrew Evans, 2009

ILLUSTRATED DICTIONARY OF CARGO HANDLING
FOURTH EDITION

By
PETER BRODIE

informa law
from Routledge

Fourth edition first published 2016
by Informa Law from Routledge
2 Park Square, Milton Park, Abingdon, Oxon OX14 4RN

and by Informa Law from Routledge
711 Third Avenue, New York, NY 10017

Informa Law from Routledge is an imprint of the Taylor & Francis Group, an Informa business

© 2016 The right of Peter Brodie to be identified as author of this work has been asserted by him in accordance with sections 77 and 78 of the Copyright, Designs and Patents Act 1988.

First edition published by Lloyd's List 1991
Third edition published by Lloyd's List 2010

All rights reserved. No part of this book may be reprinted or reproduced or utilised in any form or by any electronic, mechanical, or other means, now known or hereafter invented, including photocopying and recording, or in any information storage or retrieval system, without permission in writing from the publishers.

Trademark notice: Product or corporate names may be trademarks or registered trademarks, and are used only for identification and explanation without intent to infringe.

Lloyd's is the registered trade mark of the Society incorporated by the Lloyd's Act 1871 by the name of Lloyd's.

British Library Cataloguing in Publication Data
A catalogue record for this book is available from the British Library

Library of Congress Cataloguing in Publication Data
A catalogue record for this book has been requested

ISBN: 978-1-138-84114-7
eISBN: 978-1-315-73242-8

Typeset in 11/13 Palatino by
Servis Filmsetting Ltd, Stockport, Cheshire

To SJB

Acknowledgements

I particularly wish to thank Mr Philippe van den Kerckhove of van Doosselaere & Achten bvba, Antwerp for taking so much trouble to facilitate my visit to the various terminals and depots in Antwerp for the purpose of researching cargo handling methods and taking photographs. I must also thank personnel at the undermentioned terminals and depots for the time and trouble they took to show me round and explain the wide range of equipment they use:

– A.B.E.S n.v.
– The Cronos Group
– DP World Breakbulk Nv
– Hamilton Port Authority, Canada
– Iroquois Lock, Ontario, Canada
– Shoreham Port, UK
– Wallmann & Co., Hamburg, Germany

I acknowledge with thanks the photographs made available to me by the following organisations and for their help in the selection of suitable illustrations:

– ACL
– Canadian Coast Guard, Fisheries and Oceans Canada who supplied details and an illustration of the ice-breaker Henry Larsen.
– Cargotec Corporation for photographs of Cargotec, Kalmar, Macgregor, Moorex and Siwertell equipment
– DP World Breakbulk Nv who supplied photos in addition to showing me round their terminal
– Duluth Seaway Port Authority & Ken Newhams/Duluth Shipping News
– Euroports Belgium who also supplied photos in addition to showing me round their terminal
– The Fork Lift Truck Association Ltd for their assistance in sourcing photographs
– Linde Material Handling (UK) Ltd.
– Nemag
– Port Metro Vancouver, British Columbia, Canada
– Port of Los Angeles, California, USA
– Port of Portland, Oregon, USA

Acknowledgements

– Port of Tauranga Limited, New Zealand
– UK Met Office
– US Federal Emergency Management Association

P.B.

Preface to the fourth edition

In this edition, definitions for many of the bulk cargoes have been split to provide a fuller description of the cargo itself and, separately, methods used in handling and storage, including the type of equipment and transport used. Some cargoes have multiple illustrations showing a particular sequence of events. Some newer types of equipment have been added, as have a small number of new abbreviations.

P.B.

List of illustrations

Where a term in the dictionary has an illustration, the appropriate figure numbers are shown at the end of the definition; the number is in bold if the term is the main object being illustrated, and in italics if it is not.

1	Aggregates	2
2a	Aluminium billets bundled in 5s, each bundle weighing 5.665 tonnes	4
2b	Aluminium ingots; these are in bundles of 1 tonne and in lots of 25 tonnes as specified by the London Metal Exchange	4
2c	Superpacks of aluminium billets weighing 25 tonnes each	5
3	Automated guided vehicles at the port of Rotterdam, the Netherlands	6
4	Automatic stacking cranes; these particular cranes have a capacity of 40 tonnes, can span 10 containers and stack 6 high	7
5	Loading barley; the bottom of the loading spout is visible above the cargo	9
6	Beaufort Scale	10
7	Biomass	11
8	Block	12
9	Docks at San Pedro Bay, USA, with breakwater in the foreground	15
10a	Fertiliser in bulk bags weighing 600 kg each; at the base of each bag are diagrammatic instructions showing how to lift them and position them on pallets	16
10b	Spreaders equipped with chains and hooks for lifting bulk bags	17
11	Bulk container; this one is 9 feet high and 8 feet wide with a capacity of 35 tonnes	18
12	Fertiliser in bulk being discharged by means of a grab; note the calf dozer in the hold which is used to level the cargo in preparation for discharge	20
13	Canvas slings colour-coded to distinguish different lifting capacities	21
14	Car deck	22
15	Car sling	23
16	Clamp truck equipped with carton clamps; note the legs under	

List of illustrations

	the containers in the background which are used to raise the container to accommodate a tractor unit	25
17	Four roll trailers shown on a cassette	25
18	Cell guides	26
19	A 45-foot cellular palletwide container, 9 feet 6 inches high	27
20	Cement in bags. Each bag weighs 1.5 tonnes	28
21	Loading cement into a bulk carrier	28
22	Chain slings of various lifting capacities	30
23	Clamp truck – this one is moving aluminium billets	31
24a	Loading coal into the 'Algolake', a Great Lakes self-unloading bulk carrier	32
24b	Coal carried on a conveyor to hoppers through which rail wagons are loaded	32
25	Aerial photo of coal terminal at the port of Vancouver, Canada, showing the stacking yard, conveyor and loading of a bulk carrier	33
26	Coil mat	35
27a	Collapsible flatrack being moved by a reachstacker	36
27b	A 40-foot collapsible flatrack	36
28a	Gross, tare and net weights displayed on a 40-foot collapsible flatrack	38
28b	A 10-foot container with its doors open revealing an 8-foot container inside	39
29	Cranes loading and unloading containers from a container barge at the Port of Portland's (Oregon, USA) Terminal 6. Terminal 6 is the Columbia River's only deep-draft container terminal. Container barges like this one carry thousands of containers between Portland and upriver ports as far away as Lewiston, Idaho. The crane is rated at 50 short tons with the spreader beam and 56.5 tonnes with a hook beam	39
30	Loaded container handler	40
31	Container ramp	41
32	Container stripping boom	41
33	Fully cellular containership – this one has a capacity of 8,560 TEUs	43
34a	Paper reels being discharged onto a roll trailer using core probes	44
34b	Core probes used to discharge paper reels	45
35	Coupling of two 10-foot containers by means of an attachment to the corner castings so that they can be loaded and transported as one 20-foot container. When handled in this way, one of the container's reference numbers is covered over, and all documentation will show the other number	45
36	Pneumatic crawler crane; this model is being used to lift bales of pulp into a barge. It has a lifting capacity of 7.5 tonnes with	

List of illustrations

	a maximum reach of 20 metres. Under the load can be seen two ventilators used to ventilate the hold of the barge	47
37a	CSC plate	47
37b	CSC plate; note that this newer type is attached in one place only, for cheapness and security	48
38	Derricks	50
39	Dock leveller	51
40	Dry van container; this one is a 20-footer	54
41	Edge protector	55
42	Elephant legs	56
43	Empty container handler	56
44	Extension forks	57
45a	Portland, Oregon, USA, Terminal 5 potash export facility which handles about 2 million tons of potassium-based fertiliser each year	59
45b	Fertiliser in bulk being loaded via a mobile hopper to a truck	59
46	A 20-foot collapsible flatrack	60
47	Folding hatch covers	62
48a	Fork-lift attachment for steel coils	64
48b	These pipes, or booms, are attached to fork-lift trucks and inserted into the bore or eye of steel coils to lift them	64
49a	Fork-lift truck	65
49b	Fork-lift truck equipped with attachment for lifting steel coils. This model has a 32-tonne capacity	65
49c	Fork-lift truck equipped with low mast to enable it to be driven into shipping containers	66
50	Travelling gantry crane	68
51	Geared ship	69
52	Glass	70
	Grab types:	
53a	Clamshell grab, used for many types of bulk cargoes	71
53b	Scissors grab, higher capacity grab used for a variety of bulk cargoes	72
53c	Cactus grab, used for scrap, biomass and other shredded materials	72
53d	Trimming grab, used to remove residual loads of different types of ore. It can handle large quantities by its ability to be opened to a wide radius	73
54a	Bulk carrier loading grain stored in a dome-shaped silo via a conveyor and spout	74
54b	Port of Portland's Terminal 5 in Oregon, USA, one of the world's largest wheat export facilities. Each year about 3 million tons of grain pass through Terminal 5. Note wheat being loaded from a spout, and the ship's side-rolling hatch covers	74

List of illustrations

54c	Loading grain using a spout	75
55	Granite blocks	76
56	Guillotine door	77
57	Hand pallet truck	78
58	Side-rolling hatch covers	80
59	Heavy lift involving the use of a spreader to deal with a long and wide piece; note the elephant legs under the cargo	81
60	Heavy lift spreader in the foreground; it keeps two cranes apart while they lift a wide load in tandem	82
61	High cube cellular palletwide container; this model has compressed bamboo flooring, a recent innovation	83
62	Type of hook	84
63	Mobile hopper underneath a grab which is being used to load a free-flowing bulk cargo onto trucks	85
64	Canadian ice-breaker 'Henry Larsen'; it is a medium gulf/river ice-breaker, but also provides search and rescue support during the summer season, escorting large ships in southern Canadian waters, as well as Arctic areas, and conducts limited oceanographic, meteorological and other scientific work in regions inaccessible to conventional ships. An air bubbler system, which also acts as a side thruster, is fitted and controlled from the wheelhouse to reduce hull friction during ice-breaking operations	86
65	Rail-mounted jib cranes, Churchill Dock, Antwerp, Belgium	89
66	Cement carrier 'Alpena', one of the oldest ships trading in the Great Lakes	91
67a	Power transformer on a 170-tonne (170 tonnes carrying capacity) roll trailer; the trailer is 26 feet long; note the large circular lifting points on the left face of the transformer, and the lashing points to which chains are attached	92
67b	Interior of a 20-foot dry van container; it shows two lashing rings: one at the top, the other near the floor, three (horizontal) lashing bars and a vent next to the top lashing ring	92
68	Lift-away hatch covers	94
69	Unloading limestone	95
70	Linkspan at the port of Immingham, UK, connecting a stern ramp to the shore	95
71	Interior of a bulk container in which three roof hatches can be seen, as well as the tipping hatch at the foot of end wall	97
72	Lock. The illustration is of Iroquois Lock on the St. Lawrence Seaway. Fig. 72(a) shows the gates at one end closed. Fig. 72(b) shows the ship arrester in position in the foreground which is designed to stop a ship from hitting the lock gates if she is unable stop by herself. Fig. 72(c) shows the lock gates open. Fig.	

List of illustrations

	72(d) shows the other end of the lock with ship arrester in the foreground, curved lock gates immediately behind (these are curved to allow a current of up to 8 kph). In the background are a general purpose crane and a lift bridge in the up position, used to carry foot and motor traffic across the lock	98–99
73	Logs for export being handled at the port of Tauranga, New Zealand	100
74	Log stacker	101
75	Steel universal columns, shipped loose	102
76	Roll trailer, this one carrying aluminium billets	103
77	Label on a paper reel identifying it within a shipment of reels	104
78	Mobile crane; this model, in the Port of Antwerp, Belgium, is capable of handling cargo from ships up to Panamax size. It has a lifting capacity of 104 tonnes and a maximum radius of 48 metres. It is used for containers, dry bulk, general cargo and heavy lifts	106
79	Mobile harbour crane spreader	107
80	Self-tensioning mooring system	108
81	Narrow steel strip	109
82	Nylon round sling, used for sensitive cargoes; it has thousands of strands of fibre inside for strength	110
83a	A 40-foot open-top container	112
83b	This open-top container features a recent development: just below the soft top is one of many fixings used to support a frame which converts the top into a solid one. This provides the operator with flexibility to use the box in whichever way dictated by the nature of the cargo	112
84	Launches being loaded onto a ship; the one in the foreground is on a flatrack being moved on a roll trailer; note how the height of the launch exceeds the height of the flatrack ends	114
85	Outreach; the plate on this crane states the maximum lift at 42.5 metres is 12 tonnes and at 23.5 metres is 27 tonnes	115
86a, 86b, 86c, 86d	Packaged timber. The illustrations show packaged timber being discharged from a ship, then carried by fork-lift truck to an area of the quay to await onward transport by lorry	116–117
87	Pallet/reefer with side door equipped with a spreader and pallet cage, providing protection against the weather while loading or unloading	118
88	Pallet loading platforms; these have a safe working load of 25 tonnes each	119
89a	Pallet truck	120
89b	Pallet truck	120

xv

List of illustrations

90a	Paper clamp fitted to a clamp truck	121
90b	Paper clamp fork-lift attachment	121
90c	Older form of paper clamp still in use	122
91	Paper reels on a roll trailer	122
92	Photo gate or photo portal	125
93	Pipe hook; this one is teflon-coated, for use with coated pipes, so as not to damage the inside coating of the pipe	126
94a	Pair of plate hooks; this pair has a lifting capacity of 3 tonnes	127
94b	This spreader is being used to help lift long length steel plates; hanging from the spreader are chains linked to plate hooks	127
95	A 40-foot platform flat	128
96	The Port of Portland's (Oregon, USA) Terminal 5. In the foreground, the Portland Bulk Terminal potash export facility. In the background is Columbia Grain's Terminal 5 grain export facility	130
97	Fork-lift pulp clamp capable of lifting 2 units of 2 tonnes each x 2 high	131
98	Pure car and truck carrier in the background	132
99	Pusher tug on the Mississippi River, USA	133
100	Radiation detection system; this one is mounted on a spreader	134
101	Rail clamp; this one has a lifting capacity of 6 tonnes	135
102	Container gantry crane; this model is rail-mounted	135
103a	Reach stacker	137
103b	Reach stacker lifting a 25-tonne superpack of aluminium billets	137
104	Larger size paper reels weighing 4.5 tonnes each, with reel guards	138
105	Rear view of a refrigerated container (reefer) showing the refrigeration unit; this model is a 45-foot high cube reefer	139
106	Kiwi fruit in cartons on pallets being loaded on a refrigerated ship in Tauranga, New Zealand; the pallets are placed in pallet cages, a number of which can be seen under the hooks of the cranes	140
107a	Roll trailer; this one is 62 feet long with a 90-tonne payload	141
107b	A 220-tonne (220 tonnes carrying capacity) roll trailer, 42 feet 6 inches long	142
108	Ro-ro tractor. This model has a fifth wheel capacity of 37 tonnes	143
109	ACL ro-ro/container vessel 'Atlantic Cartier'; note the cell guides on deck	143
110	Rubber-tyred gantry cranes	144
111	Safety cage	145
112	Salt	146
113	Container security; this container has two places where seals can be affixed: the normal place is the horizontal bar, the new position is in the locking rod (the vertical bar)	148

List of illustrations

114	Self-propelled barge on the Mississippi, USA, carrying dredging pipes	149
115	Self-unloader	150
116	Separation mat	151
117	Shackles of different sizes corresponding to lifting capacities ranging from 3 tonnes to 75 tonnes	151
118	This Siwertell shiploader is totally enclosed for environment-friendly bulk handling	153
119	Shrink-wrapping	155
120	Pure car and truck carrier, the Grand Benelux; it has a capacity of 4,300 cars; its side ramp is visible amidships	156
121	Skeletal trailer	158
122	Sliding hatch covers	159
123	Chain slings	160
124a	Spreaders; the left-hand one has a lifting capacity of 25 tonnes, the right-hand one, 30 tonnes. Both are 6 metres in length	162
124b	Semi-automatic spreader; hooking (attaching the crane's hook) is automatic, unhooking is manual. It has a 70-tonne lifting capacity	162
124c	A 50-tonne spreader	162
125	Squeeze clamps	163
126a	Steel coils. These are wrapped for protection	165
126b	Attachment to a fork-lift truck for steel coils. These are teflon-coated to avoid damage to the inside of coils	165
127	Coated pipes on a rail wagon; note the wood separating the pipes to avoid damage	166
128	Steel plates	166
129	Steel rails being loaded; from the top, note the spreader, the chain slings and straps. The ship's hatch covers are folded back to allow access to the hold	167
130	Steel sheet piling; this type is known as Z-shaped, or Frodingham, piling; note the timber separations allowing a small number of bars to be lifted	168
131	Stern ramp	169
132	Straddle carrier	171
133	String of barges	172
134a	Side view of a stack of super-racks	174
134b	End view of a super-rack showing capacities	175
135	Tank containers showing how their frames enable them to be stacked in the same way as ordinary shipping containers	177
136	Reach stacker with telescopic spreader lifting a steel pipe	179
137	Terminal tractor pulling trailers with containers	180
138	Timber deck cargo	181

List of illustrations

139	Rear view of a bulk container showing the tipping hatch	182
140	Fork-lift truck with a toplift attachment equipped with a telescopic spreader	184
141	Truck sling; two slings similar to the one illustrated are together capable of lifting 25 tonnes	188
142	Turnbuckle	188
143	This example of uncontainerable cargo, which is also a heavy lift, is a power transformer being loaded onto a truck	190
144	UNIMOG – this model is based in the Port of Antwerp, Belgium	191
145a	Unloader. Siwertell ship unloaders offer record-beating capacities and are totally enclosed for environment-friendly bulk handling	192
145b	Mobile unloading system, suitable for a wide range of bulk cargoes, equipped with a covered conveyor to minimise dust. This Siwertell mobile ship unloader is the ideal solution when unloading is required in more than one spot	193
146	A bulk carrier offloads urea at the Port of Portland's (Oregon, USA) Terminal 2	194
147a, 147b, 147c, 147d	Wire rod in coil. In the illustrations, coils are being discharged from a ship onto the quay where they are lifted by fork-lift truck and placed onto an open area of ground to await onward transport by lorry.	198–199
148	Wire sling with a 1.5-tonne lifting capacity	200
149	Woodchips being transported in a barge	201

Copyright of illustrations

Copyright in the illustrations in this book belongs to the undermentioned organisations:

ACL 14, 56, 67a, 107a, 109, 120, 131

Canadian Coastguard 64

Cargotec 4, 30, 43, 47, 58, 68, 70, 80, 100, 103a, 110, 115, 118, 122, 132, 137, 145a, 145b

DP World Breakbulk 59, 143

Duluth Seaway Port Authority & Ken Newhams/Duluth Shipping News 5, 21, 24a, 54c, 66, 69, 112

FEMA News Photos 8, 38, 99, 114, 119

Linde Material Handling (UK) Ltd. 16, 44, 49a, 57, 89a, 89b, 90a, 125

Nemag 53a, 53b, 53c, 53d

Port Metro Vancouver 25, 98, 149

Port of Los Angeles 9, 87, 121

Port of Portland 29, 45a, 54b, 96, 133, 146

Port of Tauranga 12, 24b, 45b, 51, 63, 73, 74, 84, 106, 138

UK Met Office (Crown Copyright) 6

Copyright in all other photographs in the book belongs to the author.

List of abbreviations

APT After peak tank
AGV Automatic guided vehicle
BB Breakbulk
CBU Continuous barge unloader
CKD Completely knocked down
CNG compressed natural gas
COW Crude oil washing
CPC Cellular palletwide container
CPP Clean petroleum products
CSU Continuous (ship) unloader
DWAT Deadweight all told
DWCC Deadweight cargo capacity
DWT Deadweight
FEU Forty-foot equivalent unit
FPSO Floating production, storage and offloading (vessel)
FTZ Foreign-Trade Zone
FWA Fresh water allowance
GT Gross tonnage
IBC Intermediate bulk container
IGS Inert gas system
LBP Length between perpendiculars
LNG Liquefied natural gas
LOA Length overall
LPG Liquefied petroleum gas
MSL Maximum securing load
NT Net tonnage
OBO Ore/bulk/oil carrier
OO Ore/oil carrier
OOG Out of gauge
PCC Pure car carrier
PCTC Pure car and truck carriers
RFID Radio frequency identification
Ro-ro Roll-on/roll-off
RTG Rubber-tyred gantry
SBM Single buoy mooring

List of abbreviations

SBT Segregated ballast tank
SD Single deck (ship)
SWAD Salt water arrival draught
SWL Safe Working Load
TDW Total deadweight
TEU Twenty-foot equivalent unit
TPC Tonnes per centimetre
TPH Tonnes per hour
TPI Tons per inch
UBC Universal bulk carrier
ULCC Ultra-large crude carrier
VLCC Very large crude carrier
VLGC Very large gas carrier
VLOC Very large ore carrier

Abaft or **aft**   At or towards the stern or after end of a ship.

Abeam   On a line at right angles to a ship's length.

Acid tanker   Ship designed to carry acids. Its tanks are made of stainless steel or may be coated with one of a variety of linings to prevent the acid from penetrating the hull. A number of safety features are required: ventilation must be such that the crew are not affected by gases which may build up; there will also be emergency equipment to deal with breathing or contact injuries.

Aeroslide (conveyor)   *See* **Air slide conveyor**.

Aframax   Tanker in the 75,000–120,000 deadweight size range. Its name is derived from AFRA, the average freight rate assessments published by the London Tanker Brokers' Panel.

Aft   *For definition, see* **Abaft**.

Aft peak tank or **after peak tank (APT)**   Small tank situated at the extreme after end of a ship. It normally holds water ballast and is used in this way to assist in the trim of the ship, that is, the relationship of the draught forward to the draught aft.

After end   The rear of a ship.

Aggregates   Bulk cargo of various types, often crushed gravel, rock or sand, sometimes dredged from the sea, and used in the construction industry. *See Fig. 1.*

Ahead

Fig. 1 Aggregates

Ahead In advance of the ship.

Air bag Inflated bag used to fill gaps between goods when stowed in rail wagons, trucks, shipping containers or in ships. It is a means of load bracing or cushioning, the purpose being to prevent shifting of goods. In a container, for example, air bags are positioned across the length or width then inflated to brace the load against the walls or ends of the container. Air bags are also known as inflatable dunnage or dunnage bags.

Air draught One of three possible distances: (1) the maximum height from the water-line to the topmost point of a ship, that is, the superstructure or the highest mast. This information is required for ships having to navigate bridges; (2) the clearance between the topmost point of a ship and a bridge; (3) the maximum height from the water-line to the top of the hatch coamings. This figure is necessary in some bulk trades where loading is effected by conveyor belt, which projects over the hatchway. The ship must be low enough in the water, if necessary by retaining sufficient ballast on board, to allow the conveyor to clear the hatch coamings.

Air slide conveyor Type of conveyor which uses gravity to load or discharge solid bulk cargoes such as cement, and to move them from one location to another. This system uses low pressure air pumped into enclosed trunking to make the cargo behave like a fluid, a process known as fluidisation. In this way, it avoids the need for a mechanical system and is therefore quieter and needs less maintenance. The trunking is enclosed and thus suppresses dust and spillage. It is typically used to convey cement. Also known as an **aeroslide (conveyor)**. *See* **Conveyor (belt)**.

Air supported (belt) conveyor Type of belt conveyor which relies on a cushion of air to provide support to the belt, rather than the more traditional rollers. The trunking is enclosed and thus suppresses dust and spillage. This type of conveyor can transport a wide variety of bulk products, including coal, cement, sugar and sand. Also spelled **air-supported (belt) conveyor**. *See* **Conveyor (belt)**.

Alternate holds Practice of loading iron ore cargoes into every other hold on a ship, leaving the remaining holds empty. This is done because iron ore is a dense cargo and takes up relatively little space; by spreading the cargo out in this way, the ship retains structural and navigational stability.

Alumina Aluminium oxide. Extracted from bauxite, which itself is aluminium ore, it has a variety of uses including being an abrasive and a fire retardant. *See* **Alumina carrier** *and* **Alumina handling**.

Alumina carrier Specialised bulk carrier for the transport of alumina. Typically having four holds, this ship is fully enclosed because of the amount of alumina dust generated by conventional systems. Self-discharging is achieved by opening gates in the floor of the holds which allow the cargo to drop onto conveyor belts leading to one end where mechanical or pneumatic equipment elevates it to deck level. *See* **Alumina**.

Alumina handling Alumina often arrives at the loading port by rail, where there may be mechanical offloading to silos. Loading is effected by means of a chute lowered into the holds. *See* **Alumina**.

Aluminium Silver-coloured metal produced after two processes: firstly, from bauxite into alumina, and then into aluminium. It has many uses such as in packaging, including cans and foil, long-distance power lines, cladding for buildings, water treatment, medical uses and vehicle bodies. It is transported in two main forms: ingots and billets. **Aluminium ingots** resemble gold bars in form, typically moved in bundles of 1 tonne. They are traded on the London Metal Exchange in lots of 25 tonnes. **Aluminium billets** are solid cylinders, shipped typically in 5-tonne bundles or in superpacks of 25 tonnes. *See Figs. 2a, 2b, 2c, 23, 76, 103b*.

Aluminium

Fig. 2a Aluminium billets bundled in 5s, each bundle weighing 5.665 tonnes

Fig. 2b Aluminium ingots; these are in bundles of 1 tonne and in lots of 25 tonnes as specified by the London Metal Exchange

Fig. 2c Superpacks of aluminium billets weighing 25 tonnes each

Aluminium ore   *See* **Bauxite**.

Amidships   At or in the middle of the ship.

Ammonia tanker or **ammonia carrier**   Fully refrigerated tanker designed to carry ammonia in liquid form by means of refrigeration. The ammonia is carried in tanks which are kept separate from the ship's hull by an insulating barrier so as to help maintain the low temperature. Very often, ammonia tankers are also used to transport propane, a cargo which has similar requirements.

Anchorage   Place where ships drop anchor, away from shipping lanes, to wait until a loading or discharging berth becomes available, or to take bunkers from a bunker barge, or to discharge to barges, or when laid up.

Angle of repose   Angle at which a cargo settles in the hold of a ship. It is the angle between the horizontal and the slope made by a bulk cargo such as grain or iron ore. The smaller the angle, the more the cargo behaves like a liquid and the more it is likely to shift.

Apron   Hard-surfaced area of the quay on which shipping containers are assembled before loading to, or after discharging from, the ocean vessel.

Artificial tween deck

Artificial tween deck Construction made by placing several platform flats end to end in a ship. These are effectively shipping containers without sides, ends or a roof. Normally, platform flats are 20 or 40 feet long and are used to hold awkwardly shaped cargoes which cannot fit on or in any other type of container.

Asphalt tanker Ship used exclusively or predominantly to carry asphalt, a waste product of the oil refining industry. Basically a tanker, this ship has heating coils, since asphalt is viscous and solidifies unless it is kept at the correct heat.

Astern At or towards the stern of a ship.

Athwartships Across the ship, that is, from side to side. Said of cargo stowed in this way, as opposed to lengthways.

Automatic guided vehicle (AGV) or **automated guided vehicle** or **automatically guided vehicle** Vehicle of various types, used without a driver in various situations to pick up, carry and offload cargoes such as containers and pallets. Its functions are programmed in. *See Fig. 3.*

Fig. 3 Automated guided vehicles at the port of Rotterdam, the Netherlands

Automatic stacking crane Rail-mounted gantry crane which is automated to stack containers in a container terminal, so as to make the best use of space and to position containers for loading to the ship or to a vehicle. *See Fig.* **4**.

Fig. 4 Automatic stacking cranes; these particular cranes have a capacity of 40 tonnes, can span 10 containers and stack 6 high

Axial stern ramp Ramp fitted to a ro-ro ship which is situated at the rear of the ship and which opens in the direction of the ship's length. When open, this ramp connects the quay to the ship's main deck, allowing vehicles to be wheeled on and off. In some cases, there is a separate watertight door but very often the ramp itself acts as a door, when it is known as an **axial stern ramp/door.** Some ships are fitted with two stern ramps side by side.

Bagging plant Area in a terminal dedicated to loading bulk commodities into bags. It is generally more economical to load, transport and discharge bulk cargoes loose in the holds of ships. After discharge, such cargoes are put into bags for transport overland to their final destination where bags are easier to handle. *See Figs. 10a*, 20.

Bale or **bale capacity** Total cubic capacity of a ship's holds available for the carriage of solid cargo which is not capable of filling the spaces between the ship's frames. It is expressed in cubic feet or cubic metres. (Where a cargo is free-flowing and is capable of filling the spaces between the ship's frames, the corresponding cubic capacity is known as the grain or grain capacity.)

Ballast tank General term given to any tank or compartment in a ship which is used for ballast when the ship is not carrying cargo. Ballast is a heavy weight, often seawater, which gives the ship stability and improves handling. Compartments which can be used for this purpose include the double-bottom, deep tank and wing tank. When not being used for ballast, these tanks may carry fresh water, fuel or even cargo depending on the tank and the type of ship.

Banana carrier Name given to any ship dedicated to the banana trade. Such a ship is required to have considerable ventilation capability combined with the ability to cool the cargo and she must be fast because of the way bananas mature on passage. Most ships are designed to carry palletised goods although cartons are still used. Nowadays, bananas are being carried in specially designed refrigerated containers.

Banana terminal Terminal in a port dedicated to the handling and storage of bananas. Bananas are carried in cartons, often on pallets, in refrigerated ships. Modern facilities include elevators which carry the cargo to conveyor belts. Bananas may be inspected and re-palletised at the terminal before being loaded to rail or road for inland distribution.

Bar (sand) Sandbank which forms at the mouth of a river and which very often limits the size of ships able to reach up-river destinations. In many cases, ships bound for an up-river discharge port have to lighten, that is, to discharge some of their cargo to barges or small ships, before being able to navigate over a sand bar and reach the port. Equally, ships loading at an up-river port may be able to load only part of the cargo, the balance being taken on board after the ship has cleared the bar.

Barge Flat-bottomed vessel mainly used on rivers and canals. Some types are self-propelled while those which are not are pushed (pushed barges), or towed (towed barges) by a tug. Barges are often linked together and towed in a line known as a string of barges or train of barges. *See Figs*. 99, **114**.

Barge-carrying ship Ocean ship that carries barges. These barges are loaded with cargo, often at a variety of locations, towed to the ocean ship, sometimes referred to as the mother ship, and lifted or, in some cases, floated on board. After the ocean crossing, the barges are off-loaded and towed to their various locations. The ocean ship then receives a further set of barges which have been assembled in readiness. This concept was designed to eliminate the need for specialised port equipment and to avoid transhipment with its consequent extra cost.

Barley Cereal grain used in the malting and brewing industry, in the making of beer and whisky (this type of barley is known as malting barley). It is also used in food, such as breakfast cereals and noodles, as well as in baby food. Its other principal use is as an animal feed. *See* **Barley handling**.

Barley handling When shipped in bulk, barley is loaded by means of a conveyor leading to a spout which distributes it in the holds of the ship. Smaller quantities are shipped in bulk containers, and, when in bags, in general purpose containers or conventionally. Bulk cargoes are unloaded in the same way as grain, that is, by suction or grabs. *See* **Barley**. *See Fig. 5.*

Fig. 5 Loading barley; the bottom of the loading spout is visible above the cargo

Barrel handler Attachment to a fork-lift truck which is specially constructed to enable it to lift barrels. It has two sets of upper and lower clamps which hold the barrel securely. These are also capable of revolving through 90 degrees so that the barrel can be handled upright or on the roll.

Barrier seal Type of seal attached to the rods or arms on the doors of a shipping container. It is designed to stop unauthorised access. *See* **Bolt seal** *and* **Cable seal** *for types of barrier seal.*

Batten down the hatches (to) To place wooden battens over the edges of a tarpaulin which goes over the hatch beams used to cover a hatchway.

Bauxite Aluminium ore. It is processed into alumina and further processed into aluminium. It can have water added at the mine after which it moves

Beam

as slurry via a pipeline to the load port. If dry, it is transported by road and rail. At the port, bauxite is normally handled at a bulk cargo terminal, loaded by (continuous) ship loader by means of a spout, and by conventional crane using a grab. It is transported on bulk carriers and discharged by conventional cranes using grabs.

Beam The maximum breadth of a ship. This is sometimes a factor in determining whether a ship is suitable for a particular port and, consequently, whether she is suitable to be employed on a particular voyage. The beam may need to be compared with the width of locks and the outreach of cargo-handling equipment.

Beaufort Scale Scale of wind forces and sea disturbance. *See Fig. 6*.

Beaufort*	Avg Miles per Hour	Knots	Surroundings
0 calm		0 - 1	Smoke rises vertically and the sea is mirror smooth
1 light air	1.2 - 3.0	1 - 3	Smoke moves slightly with breeze and shows direction of wind
2 light breeze	3.7 - 7.5	4 - 6	You can feel the breeze on your face and hear the leaves start to rustle
3 gentle breeze	8.0 - 12.5	7 - 10	Smoke will move horizontally and small branches start to sway. Wind extends a light flag
4 moderate	13.0 - 18.6	11 - 16	Loose dust or sand on the ground will move and larger branches will sway, loose paper blows
5 fresh breeze	19.3 - 25.0	17 - 21	Surface waves form of water and small trees sway
6 strong breeze	25.5 - 31.0	22 - 27	Trees begin to bend with the force of the wind and causes whistling in telephone wires. Some spray on the sea surface
7 moderate gale	32.0 - 38.0	28 - 33	Large trees sway. Moderate sea spray
8 fresh gale	39.0 - 46.0	34 - 40	Twigs break from trees, and long streaks of foam appear on the ocean
9 strong gale	47.0 - 55.0	41 - 47	Branches break from trees
10 whole gale	56.0 - 64.0	48 - 55	Trees are uprooted and the sea takes on a white appearance
11 storm	65.0 - 74.0	56 - 63	Widespread damage
12 hurricane	75+	64 +	Structural damage on land, and storm waves at sea

Fig. 6 Beaufort Scale

Belt chain conveyor Type of continuous cargo-handling equipment consisting of a moving chain-driven belt. It is typically used for transporting grain. When used to take cargo from a ship to store or waiting transport, it is known as a belt chain unloader. Performance is measured in tonnes per hour (TPH).

Belt conveyor Type of continuous cargo-handling equipment consisting of a moving belt placed over a series of rollers, and used for a wide variety of products.

Belt unloader *See* **Belt chain conveyor**.

Berth   Place alongside a quay where a ship loads or discharges cargo or, in the case of a lay-by berth, waits until a loading or discharging berth is available. This term is also frequently used to signify a place, alongside a quay, each of which is capable of accommodating only one ship at a time.

Bilge   Area at the lower part of a hold where liquids collect and are pumped out at regular intervals.

Bilge keel   Thin plates attached to the exterior of the hull of a ship at the turn of the bilge, along part of its length. Its purpose is to deaden any rolling.

Bimodal system   Transport system whereby road trailers are coupled into trains by means of bogies and pulled on railway lines by a tractor unit. Being suitable for medium distances, this system allows tractors and trailers to be carried unaccompanied. The trailers, known as **bimodal trailers**, are standard units which need to be modified to a variable extent depending on the particular proprietary system.

Biomass   Type of recyclable material in the form of biological material in bulk form produced in particular from wood but also from agricultural or food waste. It is recycled for fuel. Biomass from wood typically takes the form of woodchips or wood pellets. It may be carried in a variety of ways, by road, rail and water, in bulk and in containers, depending on the quantity and the voyage involved. *See also* **Woodchips** *and* **Wood pellets**. *See Fig. 7.*

Fig. 7 Biomass

Bitumen carrier Specialised tanker used for the carriage of bitumen in liquid form. Bitumen solidifies at normal temperatures and so must be kept hot when being loaded and discharged as well as during the voyage. This is achieved by means of heating coils in the tanks with the temperature being monitored regularly. The ship has two longitudinal bulkheads dividing the ship lengthwise into three. Because of the temperature requirements, the cargo is carried in the centre tanks only.

Black products Crude oils, such as heavy fuel oil. Also referred to as dirty petroleum products.

Bleeding wing tank Tank, one of which is situated at each side of the top section of the holds of a bulk carrier, designed to carry free-flowing cargoes such as grain, acting as a division at the top of the stow to reduce shifting of the cargo while at sea. The cargo contained in these tanks is bled into the hold before being discharged. When not carrying cargo, this tank may be used for water ballast.

Block Device, made of wood or metal, which is part of lifting tackle equipment. It has one or more slots, each one taking a pulley wheel round which a rope passes. The pulley wheels revolve around a central pin. Blocks are typically used with derricks. *See Fig.* **8**.

Fig. 8 Block

Block stowage The placing of cargo in the hold of a ship in stacks of even length with no pieces protruding so as to make the most efficient use of the ship in the hold.

Board sling   Type of sling, that is, a piece of rope whose ends are joined together so that it forms a loop. The rope passes through holes in the four corners of a rectangular wooden board which acts as a platform for lifting goods. This type of lifting device was used in the days before containerisation.

Bogie   Wheeled undercarriage on which a container or chassis may be placed.

Bollard   Post, fixed to a quay or ship, for securing mooring rope. When on a quay, it is also referred to as a mooring post.

Bolt seal   Barrier type of seal attached to the rods or arms on the door of a shipping container, consisting of two pieces bolted together through a hole in the locking rod. A high-security device intended to prevent unauthorised access to the container. It is normally removed by means of a special tool and certain types can be re-used. Unauthorised removal is made difficult by virtue of the thickness of the bolt and, in some cases, by the seal being designed to fit close up to the door rod.

Boom (of a derrick)   The arm of a derrick which projects outward from the (upright) post and from which cargo is suspended. The boom is raised, lowered or swung by pulling or releasing ropes or chains known as guys, by means of winches.

Boom (of a fork-lift truck)   Horizontal arm that replaces the fork of a fork-lift truck. One use is to move cargoes such as pipes or coils, for example, wire rod. *See Fig.* **48b**.

Boom handler   *See* **Reach stacker**.

Bottle screw   Device that applies tension to ropes or chains used for lashing cargo. Also referred to as a turnbuckle.

Bottom side rail   Steel section running along the length of each bottom edge of a shipping container giving it structural strength.

Bottom stow cargo   Goods which are stowed at the bottom of a ship's hold because of their relatively high density, their ability to withstand other cargo being stowed on top of them and the probability that they would damage other goods if stowed elsewhere.

Bow door   Door at the forward end of a ferry which opens to allow the bow ramp to connect with the quay and enable vehicles to be driven on and off.

Bow ramp Ramp fitted to a ro-ro ship and situated at the forward end of the ship. Often this ramp acts as a watertight door when closed and is then termed a **bow door/ramp**. In order to preserve the traditional shape of the bows, ships with bow ramps have bow wing doors, which swing open and closed, or a bow visor, which is a solid structure comprising the bows; this is raised out of the way when the ramp is open.

Bow shackle Type of shackle designed to take several eyes connected to several lengths of chain. It is a piece of iron, basically V-shaped but with rounded sides. Shackles are generally used to link together two lengths of chain or a length of chain to a block, or to a mast or to the deck. They have a pin that slots through the two ends, either screwed into position or held by a device known as a forelock.

Bow thruster Small propeller near a ship's stem which is used for better manoeuvrability at low speeds.

Bow wing doors Doors at the forward end of a ferry which open to port and starboard to allow the bow ramp to connect with the quay and enable vehicles to be driven on and off. Normally, the ramp acts as a watertight door and so the wing doors do not have to fulfil this objective.

Bows Curved parts of the forward end of a ship which meet at the stem. The left bow is called the port bow and the right one the starboard bow.

Box (1) Timber box with corners strengthened with steel plates and having steel brackets underneath and around the sides for lifting purposes. It is used for handling small items which would be awkward or dangerous to lift using other means of slinging. Also known as a cargo box.

Box (2) Widely used term to designate a shipping container. *For detailed definition, see* **Container**.

Box hold vessel Vessel with a hold or holds whose sides are at right angles, or almost at right angles, to the floor. Such ships normally have wide hatchways to enable cargo to be lowered directly into the desired position in the hold. The hold is referred to as a **box hold** or **box-shaped hold**.

Box pallet Box made of four corner posts attached to four side panels made of mesh or timber. It stands on feet that enable it to be lifted by a fork-lift truck.

Breakbulk (BB) Relating to dry cargo lifted on and off ships one piece or bundle at a time by means of cranes or derricks but not shipped on trailers or in shipping containers. Such goods may be described as **breakbulk cargo**; the ships which carry them are sometimes referred to as **breakbulk ships**, which, if operated on a regular basis between advertised ports, provide a **breakbulk service**. The term breakbulk is often used to denote the opposite of containerised. Also referred to as conventional.

Breakwater   Wall built out into the sea to break the force of the waves and so protect a port from the effects of bad weather. *See Fig. 9.*

Fig. 9 Docks at San Pedro Bay, USA, with breakwater in the foreground

Bridge crane   Crane, normally a shore crane, with a wide span, used for marshalling containers and for stacking. Such cranes operate by straddling several rows of containers, placing and picking up containers as necessary. They can be either rail-mounted or rubber-tyred. They can also be fitted to certain ships, such as some self-sustaining containerships. They are also known as gantry cranes.

Bridge plate or **bridging plate**   Platform that bridges the gap between the loading bay of a warehouse and the inside of a shipping container or between the delivery bank of a shed and a rail wagon. It is also a platform on the rear of a truck that is raised or lowered to the correct height for loading or offloading.

Broken stowage   Amount of unused space in a ship or a hold by virtue of the irregular shape of the cargo. For example, the space taken up by a bundle of bars of irregular length would be calculated on the basis of the longest length, as if all the bars were of that length.

Bucket (chain) unloader

Bucket (chain) unloader Type of continuous ship unloader which consists of a big wheel with buckets that dig at the cargo in the hold, lift it out and transfer it onto a conveyor in a continuous operation. This kind of ship unloader is suitable for many types of bulk materials, including in particular coal. Performance is measured in tonnes per hour (TPH). *See* **Continuous (ship) unloader** and **Unloader**.

Bucket elevator Moving belt that brings a continuous supply of buckets loaded with bulk commodities, such as coal, to a point over the open hatchway of a ship and then empties them into the hold.

Bulbous bow Rounded projection at the forward end of a ship designed to reduce water resistance, thus allowing an increase in speed when the ship is in ballast.

Bulk bag Container, often made from polypropylene, used to carry a wide variety of bulk products, such as fertiliser, cement and sand. These bags have four loops which are hooked onto the hook of a lifting device for the purposes of loading and discharging, including placing onto, and removing from, pallets. Different bags are designed to lift different weights, from 500 kilogrammes up to 2 tonnes. They may have closures on their top surface or discharge spouts underneath, depending on the way they are used when carrying specific products. See Figs. *10a, 10b, 20*.

Fig. 10a Fertiliser in bulk bags weighing 600 kg; at the base of each bag are diagrammatic instructions showing how to lift them and position them on pallets

Bulk container

Fig. 10b Spreaders equipped with chains and hooks for lifting bulk bags

Bulk cargo Homogeneous unpacked dry cargo. Examples of bulk cargoes shipped in large quantities annually are coal, grain, woodchips and minerals. A cargo shipped in this way is said to be **in bulk**. These products are shipped in bulk carriers when in shiploads, and on containerships in bulk containers when moved in much smaller quantities. *See also* **Barley, Bulk carrier, Bulk container, Coal, Fertiliser, Grain, Salt (common salt or NaCl), Urea** *and* **Woodchips**. *See Figs. 5, 63, 71, 96, 112, 146.*

Bulk carrier Single-deck ship designed to carry homogeneous, unpacked dry cargoes such as sugar or cereals. Such ships have large hatchways to facilitate cargo-handling, hopper sides and wing tanks. The latter are used either for the carriage of grain, other bulk cargoes or water ballast. Bulk carriers, or **bulkers** as they are sometimes called, are built in a wide range of sizes and are generally gearless, although smaller vessels may have their own gear. *See Figs. 54a, 146.*

Bulk container Shipping container designed to carry free-flowing cargoes such as sugar, cement, cereals or fertilisers. The cargo is loaded through hatches in the roof of the container and discharged through a hatch in the door or front end, sometimes called a tipping hatch, by tipping the container. It may also have discharge hatches in each rear door. *See Figs. 11, 71, 139.*

Bulk discharge open-top container

Fig. 11 Bulk container; this one is 9 feet high and 8 feet wide with a capacity of 35 tonnes

Bulk discharge open-top container Shipping container resembling a full-height, open-top container, having no solid roof but instead having an open-top to enable cargoes to be loaded from the top rather than through end doors. Additionally, the bulk discharge open-top has a full-width discharge hatch, sometimes called a tipping hatch, at the front to enable bulk cargoes to be discharged by tipping the container.

Bulk newsprint carrier Ship of the bulk carrier type specially designed to carry reels of newsprint, having gantry cranes to lift the cargo on and off. A typical vessel currently trading is 15,700 tonnes deadweight with a service speed of 15 knots. It has six holds with flat-topped pontoon hatch covers and two 25-tonne rolling gantry cranes suitable for lifting 16 reels of newsprint per lift by vacuum pump. This vessel is also capable of carrying timber cargoes and containers to reduce the number of voyages in ballast.

Bulk/container carrier Multi-purpose ship designed to carry a full cargo of containers or dry bulk such as grain, coal and ore. This capability enables the ship to operate in a wider range of trades and reduces the number of voyages in ballast. It is also referred to as a container/bulk carrier. *See Fig. 11.*

Bulk-oil carrier Large multi-purpose ship, more frequently termed an ore/bulk/oil carrier. It is designed to carry cargoes either of ore or other bulk commodities or oil so as to reduce the time the ship would be in ballast if restricted to one type of commodity. The cargo is loaded into central holds and, if oil, into side tanks as well.

Bulk-ore carrier Ship designed to carry ores, having wide hatchways and a high centre of gravity. The holds are self-trimming, that is, they are shaped in such a way that the cargo levels itself. This makes such ships suitable for the carriage of grain.

Bulker *See* **Bulk carrier**.

Bulkhead Separation between compartments in a ship which may be transverse (side to side) or longitudinal (running along the length of a ship). Bulkheads contribute to the structural strength of the ship and prevent the spread of fire and seawater.

Bulkhead door Door in a ship, cut into a bulkhead, which provides access from one cargo compartment or deck to another. This is used for rolling cargo, fork-lift trucks and ship's personnel. Bulkhead doors are required to be watertight, and these may be of several types, for example, sliding, folding or pivoting.

Bulwark Part of a ship's side projecting upwards along the line of the weather deck or uppermost deck. Made of steel plates, its purpose, like a railing, is to protect people from falling overboard.

Bunker barge Barge containing bunkers used for refuelling a ship alongside a quay or at anchorage.

Buoy Small floating body, anchored to the sea bed, which marks a channel or alerts shipping to dangers, wrecks or other obstructions.

Buoy berth Buoy to which a ship is moored for the purpose of loading or discharging cargo. This could be to or from smaller craft, such as lighters. A buoy berth may be used when there is no quay or when the quay is occupied.

Buoyage The provision of buoys to mark a channel or to alert shipping to dangers, wrecks or other obstructions.

Butane carrier Ship designed to carry butane in liquid form. The butane is carried in tanks within the holds; it remains in liquid form by means of pressure and refrigeration. Such ships are also suitable for the carriage of propane.

C-hook *See* **Coil hook.**

Cable seal Barrier-type seal attached to the rods or arms on the door of a shipping container, intended to prevent unauthorised access to the container. It consists of a metal cable which is looped through the rods or arms on the doors of a shipping container and secured by being tightened through a ratchet device. It is removed by being cut and is consequently not reusable.

Cable-ship or **cable-layer** Ship designed to lay and repair power cables or communications cables on the sea bed. Cable for laying is held in tanks or holds, of which there may be several, and played out over the bows.

Calf dozer Small bulldozer used to go over bulk cargoes such as sugar for the purpose of trimming (levelling). *See Fig. 12.*

Fig. 12 Fertiliser in bulk being discharged by means of a grab; note the calf dozer in the hold which is used to level the cargo in preparation for discharge

Can hooks Set of two or more steel hooks that fit under the lip at either side of a steel drum or barrel. The hooks are linked together by a chain which tightens them on the lip of the drum or barrel when it is lifted.

Cantilever jib crane Type of mobile crane found on a truck and used, for example, to lift awkward loads into open-top containers. The jib is a long arm, normally fitted with a lifting hook, fixed to the body of the truck.

Car deck

Canvas sling Length of rope whose ends are joined together so that it forms a loop. It has a piece of canvas sewn between the parts of the rope. It is used for lifting certain bagged goods, such as grain. *See Fig. 13.*

Fig. 13 Canvas slings colour-coded to distinguish different lifting capacities

Capacity plan Document detailing the capacities of all the cargo spaces of a ship and all the tanks used for fuel oil, diesel oil, lubricating oil, fresh water and water ballast. The capacities are expressed in cubic feet or cubic metres and, in the case of the tanks, the quantity (in tons or tonnes) which they can hold.

Capesize vessel Category of bulk carrier so called because it is too large to negotiate the Suez and Panama canals. Vessels of over 150,000 tonnes deadweight fall into this category.

Car carrier Ship designed to carry unpacked cars which are driven on and off on ramps and stowed on special decks. This design arose from the increase in volume of cars being shipped internationally. Originally, ships carried cars together with other cargoes but, as numbers increased, they carried only cars on the outward leg and bulk cargoes on the return leg, for which the car decks were removed or folded away.

Car deck Deck on a ship on which vehicles are stowed when being carried between ports. Car decks can be moved out of the way when not being used to

Car ferry

give the ship operator flexibility to carry taller vehicles or other cargoes. Two basic types of movable car decks are in use: hoistable car decks are stowed under the deckhead and lowered on wires into their operational position. In some bulk carriers, hoistable decks are lowered from under the wing tanks and centre pontoons are lifted into position from their stowage position on the deck. Folding car decks are normally in two sections; when stowed, one of the sections is folded against the side of the ship, and the other under the deckhead. These are lowered by a wire into their operational position. *See Fig. 14.*

Fig. 14 Car deck

Car ferry Ship frequently used on short sea routes to carry passengers and cars. Cars are driven on and off over ramps onto one or more car decks where they are parked for the duration of the crossing. Shore operations often involve the use of a linkspan or bridge that links the ship and shore at whatever angle is necessary at the particular berth. Ferries operating on routes other than very short ones may have cabins and other passenger facilities.

Car sling Sling of various types used for lifting vehicles onto and off general cargo ships. Made of rope, or sometimes wire, this sling has a spreader from which two slings are, in turn, suspended. For lifting purposes, one of these fits under the nearside wheels of the vehicle, the other under the offside wheels. *See Fig. 15.*

Fig. 15 Car sling

Car terminal Terminal in a port dedicated to the handling of cars. Cars are driven off dedicated ships, known as car carriers or pure car carriers and parked on large parking areas. Facilities at such terminals may include de-waxing, cleaning and pre-delivery inspection, all of which is done prior to vehicles being distributed to dealers.

Cargo battens Strips of timber fixed to the frames of a ship, either in a horizontal or vertical direction, which keep cargo away from the side of the ship. This assists ventilation and helps protect against a build-up of moisture or condensation. Also known as permanent dunnage or spar ceiling.

Cargo hook Curved piece of steel, fixed to the end of a crane or derrick, to which ropes, slings or other lifting accessories placed around goods are attached for the purpose of lifting. Variations in the design exist, for example, to help prevent the hook from snagging or catching on anything while it is being raised or to stop the load from slipping.

Cargo net Device used for holding cargo while it is being lifted on and off a ship. It consists of a mesh made of rope or wire surrounded by a thicker rope or wire, used for lifting cargo. It has an eye at each corner for lifting with a

Cargo plan

hook. Only cargo which is not easily susceptible to damage can be lifted in this way. Also known simply as a net.

Cargo plan   Plan, in the form of a longitudinal cross-section of a ship, which is drawn up before loading commences. It shows suggested locations of all the consignments in the ship, taking into consideration their port of destination and their safety in transit as well as the safety of the ship. A cargo plan is often taken to be synonymous with a stowage plan since the latter has the same format but shows the actual locations of all the consignments once they have been stowed in the ship.

Cargo sweat   Condensation that occurs when a ship sails from a cool to a relatively warm climate. The temperature of the cargo rises at a slower rate than that of the ship's environment and when the surface of the cargo is colder than the dew point of the surrounding air, moisture condenses directly onto the cargo. Opinions differ as to whether the cargo should be ventilated when meeting these climatic conditions, so as to avoid damage caused by cargo sweat.

Cargo tank   Ship's tank used for the carriage of cargo, as opposed to, for instance, a ballast tank.

Cars   Cars (automobiles) are delivered by trailer or road car carrier to and from the load and discharge port respectively, may be driven there, or may be carried in containers. Cars were traditionally carried conventionally, had a sling placed around them at the load port and were lifted onto the ship by conventional crane. In recent years, new cars have been transported in large numbers around the world on dedicated ships known as car carriers (*see* **Car carrier**). Smaller numbers or individual vehicles, including second-hand cars, are often shipped in containers (*see* **Cars in containers**). *See also* **Car deck**, **Car ferry**, **Car sling** *and* **Car Terminal**.

Cars in containers   Small numbers of cars, and second-hand cars, are often shipped in shipping containers. They are driven into the container on ramps made of steel or wood, and lashed so they do not move when in transit. Some containers have an internal ramp allowing two cars to be loaded into a 20-foot container, one car partially above the other, and four cars in a 40-foot box. Within the container, the upper level consists of a platform which may be integral to the ramp or may be separate. *See* **Cars**.

Carton clamps   Attachments to a fork-lift truck that enable it to grip and lift cartons from the two sides. They take the form of large square or rectangular pads of various sizes. Using carton clamps avoids the need to have cartons placed on pallets. *See Fig. 16.*

Fig. 16 Clamp truck equipped with carton clamps; note the legs under the containers in the background which are used to raise the container to accommodate a tractor unit

Case dogs or **case hooks** Pair of clamps that fit on either side of a wooden box or crate, used for lifting. Each clamp or hook has small spikes which bite into the wood and help in gripping the crate.

Cassette Type of trailer resembling a flatrack used to convey cargoes, such as reels of paper or steel coils onto and off ro-ro ships. It is lifted onto a trailer, known as a **cassette trailer**, and towed by a tractor unit which is part of the port terminal's facilities. The cassettes are placed on vehicle decks and towed off at destination, after which the cargo is transferred to other means of transport such as road trailers or rail wagons. *See Fig.* **17**.

Fig. 17 Four roll trailers stored on a cassette

Cassette carrier

Cassette carrier Ship designed for the carriage of cassettes (*see* **Cassette**). It has decks similar to the car decks of ro-ro ships, with bulkheads positioned at intervals to prevent the shifting of the cassettes while in transit.

Cattle carrier Ship used for the carriage of live cattle. Many are converted from oil tankers and dry cargo ships of various types, although a few have been purpose-built. Cattle are loaded and unloaded along ramps and carried in pens on several decks, all of which are weather-protected. The pens have troughs for feed and water. Some deck space is set aside for the carriage of hay, for which the ship may be equipped with a dedicated crane.

Ceiling Timber placed across the floor of the cargo hold of a ship to protect it from damage.

Cell Compartment in the hold of a containership into which a shipping container fits exactly. Also referred to as a slot.

Cell guide One of the four uprights comprising a cell in a containership into which a container fits exactly. These uprights hold the container in position. *See Fig. 18.*

Fig. 18 Cell guides

Cement

Cellular barge Barge dedicated to the carriage of shipping containers and fitted with cell guides similar to those in cellular containerships.

Cellular containership Ship that is dedicated to the carriage of shipping containers: it is fitted with cell guides, uprights which provide a framework designed to accommodate standard size containers in such a way that the containers do not move in any direction. Containers are normally carried both under deck, covered with hatch covers, and on deck. *See Fig. 33.*

Cellular double bottom Space between the floor of a ship's holds and the bottom of the ship. Its purpose is to help prevent sea water entering the holds in the event of the ship running aground. Made up of several compartments, it is used for the carriage of fuel oil or fresh water or, if the ship is not carrying a cargo, for water ballast.

Cellular palletwide container (CPC) Shipping container designed to carry an optimum number of europallets. To achieve this, modern versions have a thinner wall than a standard container to achieve a greater internal width. *See Figs. 19, 61.*

Fig. 19 A 45-foot cellular palletwide container, 9 feet 6 inches high

Cement Very widely used, mainly in the production of concrete for the building industry, and for such end uses as the lining of cast iron pipes used

27

Cement carrier

in the water industry. Raw materials, typically limestone, chalk, clay and iron ore, which make up cement, are quarried; chemicals are added, and the resulting mixture ground into powder. Gypsum is added to control the setting time, together with other elements. *See also* **Cement carrier**, **Cement handling** *and* **Cement terminal**. *See Figs. 20, 21.*

Fig. 20 Cement in bags. Each bag weighs 1.5 tonnes

Cement carrier Type of bulk carrier specially designed for the carriage of cement. Self-unloading ships, they have one or more conveyor belts running fore and aft which carry the cargo to the stern where one of the several means of elevating bring the cargo to deck level where it is transferred to a boom for discharging. Because of the problems with dust, special terminal facilities are required. Cement is also carried on general cargo ships and small bulk carriers. *See* **Cement**. *See Figs. 21, 66.*

Fig. 21 Loading cement into a bulk carrier

Cement handling Cement is carried overland by rail and road between the plant and the load port, and between the discharge port and the final destination. When carried in bulk, it can be transported by train in a variety of rail wagons, mainly tank wagons and hopper wagons; when carried by road, bulk containers or tank containers are used; if in bags, it is sometimes carried in general purpose containers. At the load port, the cargo is transferred to a storage facility, often a silo, pending the arrival of the ocean vessel. It is then taken by conveyor to the ship and loaded in a variety of ways depending on the facilities at the port. This could typically be by conveyor or might be by grab. At the discharge port, cement carriers use their own equipment to discharge the cargo. Other types of ship use a variety of shore equipment, either conveyors or grabs. *See* **Cement**.

Cement terminal Terminal in a port dedicated to the handling and storage of cement. Facilities at the terminal may include bagging equipment. *See* **Cement**.

Centre tank Tank in a tanker which is the middle one of three tanks viewed across the ship. The two tanks on either side are designated side tanks or wing tanks. Not all tankers are divided longitudinally into three but, where this is so, either the centre tank is the largest or else all three are of equal size.

Centre-line bulkhead Vertical separation in the holds of a ship which runs lengthways along a ship, except underneath the hatchways. This type of bulkhead is constructed in order to provide the ship with additional longitudinal strength.

Centrifugal thrower Machine which receives dry bulk cargo often by means of a hopper and in which the precipitating jet revolves through 360 degrees, so that the stream of bulk cargo is distributed in all directions. It is used for stowing sugar, ores and minerals in the holds of bulk carriers and in warehouses.

Chain sling Length of chain mainly used for putting around logs or some steel products, such as beams and columns, to enable them to be lifted by crane onto and off ships. The chain has a ring at one end and a hook at the other. *See Figs. 22, 123*.

Chassis

Fig. 22 Chain slings of various lifting capacities

Chassis   Trailer on which shipping containers are carried when moved by road. There are two commonly available types: one for 20-foot containers, the other for 40-foot containers. Some 40-foot chassis are optionally able to carry two 20-foot containers.

Chemical tanker   Tanker designed to carry liquid chemicals, such as acids, in bulk. Because of the necessity to ensure quality control for many chemicals, tanks in a chemical tanker are often coated or constructed of stainless steel. Depending on the type of cargo expected to be carried, these ships may be equipped with heating coils.

China clay   *See* **Kaolin**.

Chock (to)   To place pieces of dunnage in between pieces of cargo or between the cargo and, for example, a bulkhead in order to prevent shifting of the cargo during a sea passage.

Clam-shell grab   Grab with two parts or buckets, slung under a conventional crane. The parts are brought together to lift a bulk cargo.

Clamp   Lifting device attached to a crane. The basic operation is the tensioning of grips placed in or around the cargo to be lifted. Clamps are of varying types according to the nature of the cargo: for example, probe clamps are designed to lift reels of paper, the probes being inserted into the bore of the reels before being tensioned; plate clamps are placed along the edges of steel plates and these grip the plates as they are lifted. *See Fig. 90c.*

Clamp truck Type of terminal truck used to handle various types of product, including barrels, drums, cartons and reels, especially paper reels. It is fitted at the front with two clamps which hold the cargo, then raise it so that it may be moved from one location to another, either within a warehouse or between the warehouse and the quay. In the case of paper reels, the clamps are curved to fit the shape of the reel; the pressure of the clamps on the reel may be preset, or, in the case of modern so-called intelligent clamp trucks, may be determined by an on-board computer. This is so that the reel does not get squeezed if the pressure is too great or slip if insufficient. *See Figs.* **16, 23, 97**.

Fig. 23 Clamp truck – this one is moving aluminium billets

Clean petroleum products (CPP) or **clean products** Refined products such as aviation spirit, motor spirit and kerosene. Also referred to as white products.

Cleaning the holds Sweeping the holds of a ship and, if necessary, washing them down after a cargo has been discharged so that they are clean in readiness for the next cargo. It is often a requirement of time charter-parties that the holds of the ship be clean or swept clean on delivery to the time charterer at the beginning of the period of the charter and, similarly, on redelivery to the shipowner at the end of the charter.

Clip-on unit Generator that can be attached to a refrigerated container to provide auxiliary power. *See also* **Generator set**.

Coal Fossil fuel which is used in very large quantities worldwide in electricity generation, iron and steel production, cement manufacturing and as a liquid fuel. Some coal cargoes are prone to spontaneous combustion due to oxidisation which requires special precautions. *See also* **Coal handling**. *See Figs.* ***24a, 24b, 53a.***

Fig. 24a Loading coal into the 'Algolake', a Great Lakes self-unloading bulk carrier

Fig. 24b Coal carried on a conveyor to hoppers through which rail wagons are loaded

Coal handling At a coal-loading port, coal is delivered by road, rail or barge, depending on the distances and locations involved, and stored in stacks awaiting the carrying ship. One recent development is to transport coal to the load port by containers for environmental reasons. At the coal terminal at the loading port, it is normally loaded to a belt conveyor by means of a stacker/reclaimer, which is equipment consisting of multiple buckets which scoop the coal continuously onto the conveyor. It is fed into the ship's holds by a shiploader equipped with a spout. At the coal terminal at the discharge port, it is discharged by grab through hoppers onto trucks or rail wagons. Sometimes the coal is transported away from the quay on a conveyor and then loaded to rail. *See also* **Bucket (chain) unloader, Collier, Grab type ship unloader** *and* **Screw conveyor**. *See Fig. 25.*

Fig. 25 Aerial photo of coal terminal at the port of Vancouver, Canada, showing the stacking yard, conveyor and loading of a bulk carrier

Coaming Steel surround to a hatchway, which rises vertically from the deck of a ship. Its functions are to prevent water washing into the hold and to lessen the risk of any person who may be working on the deck falling through the open hatchway. Also known as a hatch coaming.

Coaster Ship which carries cargoes between ports on the same coast or ports of the same country. This term is also used occasionally to refer to short sea traders, that is, ships which perform short international voyages. There is no real distinction in terms of construction between the two – ships in either trade are of very varied types: they may have one deck or more than one, they may be geared or gearless, they may have one hatch or several and may be fitted to carry containers. As a rule, they are small in relation to ocean-going vessels.

Coffee Product shipped worldwide in an unroasted state, when it is known as green coffee. *See* **Coffee handling** *and* **Coffee terminal**.

Coffee handling Coffee is shipped in bulk and in bags. The bags are normally made of jute or sisal. Coffee is increasingly shipped in containers: general purpose or ventilated containers when the cargo is in bags, and in bulk containers when it is moved unpacked. *See* **Coffee** *and* **Coffee terminal**.

Coffee terminal Terminal in a port dedicated to the handling and storage of coffee. Storage of bulk coffee is in silos, whereas the bags are stored in warehouses. Facilities at such terminals may include cleaning, dust removal, palletisation and blending.

Cofferdam Part of the construction of a ship, particularly tankers, consisting of bulkheads arranged in such a way that they form a hollow subdivision between cargo compartments. This, for example, provides a measure of protection against mixing of products or different grades carried in adjacent tanks. Similarly, extra protection is obtained when a cofferdam is constructed between cargo compartments and the engine room.

Coil carrier Shipping container, resembling a flatrack, which has a depression known as a well in which steel coils rest to prevent them from moving when in transit. Sometimes called a **coil carrier cassette.**

Coil hook Large hook, attached to a crane, used to lift and stack steel coils. The tine of the hook is inserted into the bore of the coil for lifting. Sometimes termed a C-hook because of its shape, it can be used in pairs.

Coil mat Steel matted sling used to lift steel coils. It is positioned through the bore, or 'eye', of the coil then the rings at each end are attached to a hook for lifting. Coil mats come in various capacities, representing the maximum weight of coil which can be lifted. *See Fig. 26.*

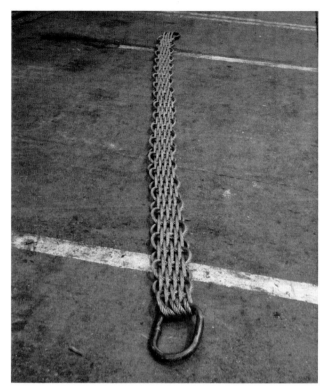

Fig. 26 Coil mat

Coil tongs   Large lifting device for steel coils. There are various types with different lifting capacities, falling into two main categories: those which lift the coil on the roll (with the bore horizontal), and those which lift the coil 'eye to sky' (with the bore vertical).

Coiling hatch cover   Type of hatch cover which consists of several panels which are coiled, when opened, around a drum, situated at the end of the hatch. A variety of this hatch cover consists of a corrugated sheet which coils when open, the corrugations nesting on top of each other, thus taking up as little space as possible around the drum. This hatch cover is used on barges as well as road vehicles and rail wagons.

Collapsible flatrack   Shipping container, consisting of a flat bed and solid ends but with open sides, designed to carry cargoes of awkward size. When these flatracks are empty, the ends are folded down and several flatracks may then be interlocked in a stack that has the same dimensions as a single standard container, enabling them to be transported in the same way. Also called a folding flatrack. *See Figs.* **27a, 27b, 46.**

Collapsible flatrack

Fig. 27a Collapsible flatrack being moved by a reachstacker

Fig. 27b A 40-foot collapsible flatrack

Collapsible mast Ship's mast which is capable of being folded down to enable the ship to pass under a bridge or a series of bridges.

Collier Type of bulk carrier purpose-built for the carriage of coal. Normally with three, four or five holds, it has large hatchways to give rapid discharge by allowing the grabs easy access to all parts of the holds. Loading is effected by gravity from chutes. Some colliers have conveyor belts for discharging in which case they are said to be self-unloaders.

Combinable cranes Two ship's cranes which can be employed together so as to make use of their combined lifting capacity when handling lifts in excess of their individual capacities.

Combination carrier Ship whose construction allows the carriage of either bulk cargoes, such as ore, or cargoes of oil. The purpose is to reduce the amount of time a ship would spend in ballast, that is, without a cargo, if she were only capable of carrying one type of cargo. Additionally, such ships are able to select the commodity that provides the best return. Examples of combination carriers are ore/oil carriers and ore/bulk/oil carriers.

Completely knocked down (CKD) Said of a cargo, normally of cars, that is shipped in pieces and cased, to be assembled at destination.

Compressed natural gas carrier Ship designed to carry compressed natural gas (CNG), a product which has been compressed such that it can be carried in pressure vessels. It is known as a CNG carrier.

Conair container Refrigerated container whose cooling is achieved by means of air blown through a flue from a central ventilation system in the ship.

Conbulker *See* **Container/bulk carrier.**

Condensation Turning of water vapour into liquid, which occurs when a ship sails from a cool to a relatively warm climate (*see* **Cargo sweat**) or from a warm to a relatively cool climate (*see* **Ship's sweat**). Often the expert use of ventilation is required to prevent condensation which can cause serious damage to cargoes. It may be possible to coat the ship's surfaces with a product that prevents condensation from dripping onto cargo.

Cone Device for positioning one shipping container on top of another using the corner castings. This is necessary on ships having no cell guides. Also known as a locating cone or a stacking cone.

Con-ro ship Ship which is designed to carry both shipping containers and ro-ro cargo. It has cell guides within which to accommodate the containers

Constants

and also has decks to take ro-ro cargo. Also known as a ro-ro/container vessel.

Constants Combined weight of a ship's stores and spares. This weight, normally expressed in tons or tonnes, is taken into consideration when calculating the maximum quantity of cargo, bunkers and fresh water which the ship can lift.

Contact inhibitor Substance, such as sodium benzoate, which is used in conjunction with packaging to inhibit corrosion to ferrous metals and some non-ferrous metals. The method of application is to impregnate the packaging, which may be a waterproof paper, with the contact inhibitor and to ensure that all the surfaces of the cargo are in contact with the packaging. This is designed to prevent water or condensation from reaching the goods themselves.

Container Box designed to enable goods to be sent from door to door without the contents being handled. There are several standard sizes used worldwide such that the same container may be transferred from one mode of transport to other modes in the course of a single voyage. Indeed, specially designed road and rail vehicles and special ships are widely used to carry containers. The most common sizes of containers are the 20-footer, which measures about 20 feet (6.1 metres) long by 8 feet (2.4 metres) wide by 8 feet 6 inches (2.6 metres) high and the 40-footer, measuring about 40 feet (12.2 metres) long and having the same width and height as the 20-footer. Typically made of steel, there are containers of several types whose use depends principally on the nature of the cargo, for example dry bulk, liquid or perishable cargoes. The different types of container are described elsewhere in this dictionary. The container is widely referred to as a box. *See Figs.* **11**, **19**, *28a*, **28b**, *33*, **35**, **40**, **61**, *67b*, *71*, **83a**, *83b*, **105**, *113*, **135**, **139**.

Fig. 28a Gross, tare and net weights displayed on a 40-foot collapsible flatrack

Container barge

Fig. 28b A 10-foot container with its doors open revealing an 8-foot container inside

Container barge   Barge designed, or utilised, to carry shipping containers. Barges dedicated to the carriage of containers are fitted with cell guides similar to those found in cellular containerships. Such barges are known as cellular barges. *See Fig. 29.*

Fig. 29 Cranes loading and unloading containers from a container barge at the Port of Portland's (Oregon, USA) Terminal 6. Terminal 6 is the Columbia River's only deep-draught container terminal. Container barges like this one carry thousands of containers between Portland and upriver ports as far away as Lewiston, Idaho. The crane is rated at 50 short tons with the spreader beam and 56.5 tonnes with a hook beam

Container berth

Container berth Place alongside a quay where containerships load and discharge. It is normally equipped with cranes, tractors and trailers and straddle carriers for moving the containers to and from the stacking areas.

Container capacity Total number of shipping containers, generally expressed as the number of TEUs (20-foot equivalent units), which may be accommodated on board a ship.

Container freight station Place where consignments are grouped together and packed into a shipping container, or a place where such consignments are unpacked. Container freight stations handle deliveries and collections by road and very often by rail as well. They are located in and around ports, as distinct from inland container depots, which perform the same function but which are generally located in the hinterland.

Container handler Name given to any truck dedicated to handling shipping containers in a port or terminal. The most common type is the frontlift truck. Also known as a top pick. *See Fig. 30.*

Container head The end without doors of a shipping container.

Container on flatcar North American expression for the method of transporting a shipping container on a flatcar, which is a rail wagon with a flat bed.

Fig. 30 Loaded container handler

Container port Port whose only, or principal, traffic is cargo in shipping containers. Its berths are equipped with container cranes, and there are large areas for stacking the containers prior to loading onto the ship or after discharging.

Container ramp Ramp used to enable a fork-lift truck to drive into a shipping container. *See Fig. 31.*

Fig. 31 Container ramp.

Container ship *See* **Containership**

Container stripping boom Attachment to a fork-lift truck which enables the fork-lift to be driven into a container for the purposes of unloading it. The cargo is placed on the boom and the fork-lift reverses out of the container with the cargo. *See Fig. 32.*

Fig. 32 Container stripping boom

Container terminal Part of a port where containers are loaded onto, and discharged from, containerships.

Container yard Place to which full container loads are delivered by the shipper to the ocean carrier and to which empty containers are returned.

Containerable or **containerisable** Said of cargo which is capable of being loaded into a shipping container.

Container/barge carrier Ship designed to carry barges and shipping containers at the same time. The barges are floated into the ship through large bow doors. The containers are stowed on deck.

Container/bulk carrier Multi-purpose ship designed to carry a full cargo of containers or dry bulk such as grain, coal and ore. This capability enables the ship to compete in a wide range of trades and reduces the number of voyages in ballast. Certain holds may be left empty as required for some dense cargoes, and all holds are shaped to facilitate discharge by grabs. Also known as a conbulker.

Container/pallet carrier Ship designed to carry shipping containers and palletised goods. Although the ship is capable of carrying general cargo, the interior of the ship generally carries paper products on pallets. These are loaded through a side door, taken by pallet lift to the appropriate level and thence by a fork-lift truck to the desired positions. The containers are carried on deck. This type of vessel is sometimes called a pallet carrier.

Containership Ship specially designed to carry shipping containers. It has cells into which the containers are lowered and where they are held in place by uprights called cell guides. Larger ships are gearless, relying on high-capacity shoreside cranes. Smaller feeder containerships often have their own cranes so that they can trade at ports with inferior, or no, cranes. Containerships have become progressively larger since they were introduced in the 1960s. Successive classes, or generations as they have been called, have seen increases in length, width, draft and carrying capacity: the first generations had capacities of about 1,000 TEUs, getting progressively larger until the fifth generation with ships of 6,000–10,000 TEUs. Currently, the largest ship has a capacity of over 15,000 TEUs. Also spelled **container ship**. *See Figs. 18, 33.*

Fig. 33 Fully cellular containership – this one has a capacity of 8,560 TEUs

Contamination (of cargo) Tainting of cargo by virtue of its being stowed in close proximity to a product with a strong odour or in a compartment that previously contained such a product and which has not been cleaned. Some commodities are susceptible to being damaged in this way; one example is tea.

Continuous ship loader Generic name for an uninterrupted and normally automated loading system for bulk cargoes into the holds of a ship. Sometimes spelled **continuous shiploader**.

Continuous (ship) unloader (CSU) *and* **continuous barge unloader (CBU)** Generic name for an uninterrupted and normally automated unloading device for bulk cargoes from the hold of a ship or barge respectively. There are two main types: mechanical and pneumatic. *For mechanical unloaders, see* **Belt chain conveyor** *and* **Bucket (chain) unloader**. *See also* **Pneumatic unloader**. Performance is measured in tonnes per hour (TPH).

Controlled atmosphere (CA) container Special shipping container used to transport perishable goods. Gases, temperature and humidity are controlled in order to slow down the degradation or ripening of the goods.

Conventional Relating to dry cargo lifted on and off ships, one piece or bundle at a time, by means of cranes or derricks but not shipped on trailers or in shipping containers. Such goods may be described as **conventional cargo**; the ships which carry them are sometimes referred to as **conventional ships**

Conveyor (belt)

which, if operated on a regular basis between advertised ports, provide a **conventional service**. Also referred to as breakbulk.

Conveyor (belt) Moving strip along which goods are moved vertically, horizontally or along an incline to deliver them from one area, such as a loading bay, into a warehouse. Certain bulk cargoes, such as coal particularly, are delivered along conveyor belts from a hopper to the ship where they are fed into spouts. These are then directed into the appropriate part of the ship. There are two main types, each of which has variants: the screw conveyor and the belt conveyor. The belt conveyor can be chain-driven or can use air in two ways: the air slide conveyor, otherwise known as the aeroslide conveyor, and the air supported conveyor. Conveyors may be fixed or mobile and each type has variants. *See* **Air slide conveyor, Air supported (belt) conveyor, Belt conveyor** *and* **Screw conveyor.**

Convoy Group of ships escorted along a stretch of water. For instance, on a canal which is not wide enough for ships sailing in opposite directions to pass each other, the most efficient solution is for ships to transit in convoy, first in one direction, and then the other.

Core probe Length of tube, often tapering, inserted into the 'eye', or core, of a roll, in particular, a paper reel, in order to lift it without needing to touch and possibly damage the exterior. It has an expanding mandrel which opens out mechanically once inside the core for the purpose of gripping. *See Figs. 34a, 34b*.

Fig. 34a Paper reels being discharged onto a roll trailer using core probes

Corner casting

Fig. 34b Core probes used to discharge paper reels

Corner casting or **corner fitting** Fitting located at each of the corners of a shipping container by means of which the container is handled and lifted. *See Fig. 35.*

Fig. 35 Coupling of two 10-foot containers by means of an attachment to the corner castings so that they can be loaded and transported as one 20-foot container. When handled in this way, one of the container's reference numbers is covered over, and all documentation will show the other number

Corner post Steel section that runs along the edge of a shipping container between the bottom and top rails, one at each corner of the container.

Corner protector Rigid construction used normally in a warehouse to protect the corner of a stack of goods from damage caused by vehicles such as fork-lift trucks. It covers the corner formed by the two outward facing sides of the goods. It may also be used to protect a load from being damaged by the strapping. Edges and corners are the most vulnerable parts of a product or packaging.

Corresponding draught Depth to which a ship is immersed in water corresponding to a particular deadweight, that is, when carrying a particular quantity of cargo, fuel, fresh water and stores.

Corrugated container Type of shipping container, made of steel, which has corrugated sides, ends and roof to give it additional structural strength.

Coselle Proprietary method of transporting compressed natural gas (CNG), which is essentially a large coil or carousel of pipe wound into a cylindrical storage container. Several of these containers are carried aboard a dedicated vessel. The gas is compressed at the terminal in the country of destination.

Cotton hooks or cotton dogs Pair of hooks linked together and attached to a crane. They are used, as their name suggests, for lifting bales of cotton or similar goods.

COW *See* **Crude oil washing.**

Crane Machine for lifting and moving heavy weights. Cranes may be mobile (on wheels or tracks), floating or fixed to the shore or to the deck of a ship (*see individual entries*). Operationally, the important features are the maximum allowable lift, referred to as the 'safe working load' and the outreach or distance outwards which the crane can reach for picking up or putting down cargo. *See Figs. 4, 36, 65, 78, 102*.

Crawler crane or **crawler mounted crane** Type of mobile crane mounted on crawlers or tracks. It may have a specific use, such as one fitted with a grab, or it may be multi-functional, having the capability to be fitted with a hook, grab or drag-line. *See Fig. 36*.

CSC Plate

Fig. 36 Pneumatic crawler crane; this model is being used to lift bales of pulp into a barge. It has a lifting capacity of 7.5 tonnes with a maximum reach of 20 metres. Under the load can be seen two ventilators used to ventilate the hold of the barge

Cross member or **cross bearer** Steel section, one of several running from one bottom side rail of a shipping container to the other, contributing to its structural strength.

Crude oil washing System of cleaning the tanks of a tanker by washing them with the cargo of crude oil while it is being discharged.

CSC Plate Plate attached to a shipping container which shows that it has been inspected and complies with the International Convention for Safe Containers in respect of handling, stacking and transport. *See Figs. 37a, 37b.*

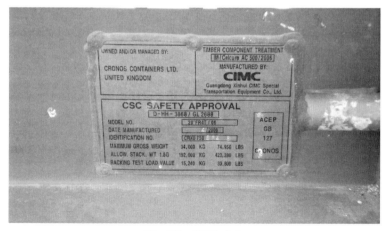

Fig. 37a CSC plate

47

Curtain-sided truck

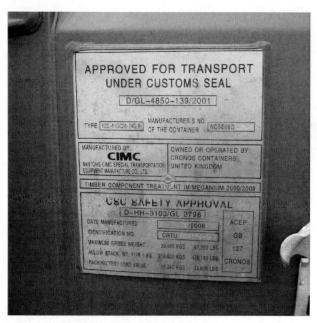

Fig. 37b CSC plate; note that this newer type is attached in one place only, for cheapness and security

Curtain-sided truck Truck which has curtains or heavy screens covering both sides. These can be folded away when the vehicle is being loaded or off-loaded. Like an open-side container, this truck is used where side access is necessary.

Dangerous goods Cargo which is potentially hazardous, such as inflammable or toxic goods. Such cargo must be notified by the shipper to the shipping company as being dangerous and is usually carried on deck. Also known as hazardous materials or hazardous goods.

Dangerous goods terminal Dedicated terminal in a port for receiving, storing and loading dangerous goods. Safety is paramount and such terminals are equipped with fire-resistant walls, sprinkler systems and good ventilation. Terminals have separate compartments for different products and may have bottling plants.

Data plate Plate fixed on a shipping container specifying its tare and gross weight. The gross weight should not be exceeded.

Deadweight (DWT) or deadweight all told (DWAT) Difference between a ship's loaded and light displacements, consisting of the total weight of cargo, fuel, fresh water, stores and crew which a ship can carry when immersed to a particular load line, normally its summer load line. The deadweight is expressed in tons or tonnes. Also referred to as total deadweight.

Deadweight cargo Cargo one tonne of which measures one cubic metre or less. Freight on deadweight cargo is generally payable on the weight, that is, per tonne or per ton. Also referred to as weight cargo.

Deadweight cargo capacity (DWCC) or **deadweight carrying capacity** Weight of cargo that a ship is able to carry when immersed to the appropriate load line, expressed in tonnes or tons.

Deadweight scale Table which shows in columns a set of draughts with a ship's corresponding deadweight tonnages when it is lying in salt water and fresh water. The table also shows the quantity of cargo, expressed in tonnes per centimetre or tons per inch, needed to immerse the ship one further centimetre or inch. This quantity varies not only ship by ship but also according to the quantity already on board.

Deballast (to) To remove the ballast from a ship. In the case of water ballast, this entails pumping it overboard.

Deck Covering of all or part of the hull of a ship into which hatchways are cut to give access to the holds.

Deck cargo Cargo carried on the open deck of a ship. Cargoes traditionally carried in this way include dangerous goods, timber and goods which are too large for the hatchways. Considerations needed when contemplating carrying cargo on deck are the strength of the deck; the strength of the hatch covers if cargo is stowed on top of them; the safety of the crew and their ability to go from one part of the ship to another; and the need to ensure that cargo is not stacked so high as to impede navigation. Deck cargo is normally carried at the risk of cargo interests.

Deck line Line 12 inches or 300 millimetres long, painted amidships on both sides of a ship and parallel to the load lines. This line is located at the point where the uppermost continuous deck, known as the freeboard deck, meets the side of the ship. The distances between the deck line and each of the load lines represent the ship's minimum freeboards allowable in various load line zones.

Deck-house Superstructure found on the upper deck of a ship and which does not extend across the full breadth of the ship.

Deep tank

Deep tank Tank situated between the holds of a ship, primarily used for water ballast but capable of carrying water or fuel.

Depth moulded Vertical distance from the keel to the uppermost deck, taken inside the ship's plating. Also, when a particular deck is specified, the depth moulded is the vertical distance to that deck. Also referred to as moulded depth.

Derrick Lifting equipment on board a ship. It consists of an upright post attached to the deck and an inclined spar or boom. The boom is supported by ropes or chains called guys. Cargo is lifted on a hook suspended from a line termed a fall. Manipulation of lines is achieved by winches. Two principal methods are adopted for lifting cargo: one is the use of two derricks whereby one is located over the hold, the other over the quay or lighter; this is known as union purchase. The other method involves only one derrick, a swinging derrick, which is swung between the ship and the shore or lighter. Derricks have a safe working load, varying from one derrick to another; this applies to their use singly and should never be exceeded. *See Fig. 38.*

Fig. 38 Derricks

Destuff (to) To unload a shipping container. Also referred to as to strip.

Dew point Temperature at which condensation first occurs and moisture is formed. If the temperature of the outside air falls below that within a confined

Dock leveller

space such as the hold of a ship or a shipping container, moisture forms on the interior steelwork of the ship or container. If, on the other hand, the temperature of the outside air rises above that of the interior of the ship or container, moisture forms directly on the cargo. It is necessary in certain circumstances to ventilate a ship's hold in order to change the dew point temperature, thus avoiding condensation.

Dirty petroleum products Crude oils, such as heavy fuel oils. Also referred to as black products.

Discharging hatch Opening in the door or front end of a shipping container through which a bulk cargo is unloaded when the container is tipped.

Displacement scale Table which shows in columns a set of draughts with a ship's corresponding displacement tonnages when it is lying in salt water and fresh water.

Displacement or **displacement tonnage** Weight of water displaced by a ship.

Dock Enclosed basin surrounded almost completely by quays used for loading and discharging ships. See *Fig. 9*.

Dock leveller Type of ramp which bridges the gap between a trailer-mounted shipping container and a loading bank. It is shaped to allow for the difference in height of the two surfaces. *See Fig. 39*.

Fig. 39 Dock leveller

Docker's hook Curved piece of steel with a point, held in the hand by a docker and used to attach to sacks of cargo for the purpose of moving them from place to place, both on shore and in the hold of a ship. Also known as a stevedore's hook or hand hook, as distinct from a cargo hook, which is attached to a crane or derrick.

Dogs Pairs of hooks used for handling and lifting various types of material. Examples are case dogs, used for wooden cases or crates, and cotton dogs, used for bales of cotton.

Dolphin Island mooring generally constructed of wooden piles or cement blocks.

Door Section of a ship which is used to provide a means of entry for vehicles into a ro-ro vessel. Sometimes the door and the access ramp for vehicles are combined while in other cases the two are separate. In most cases, the door provides a watertight barrier against the entry of seawater.

Door gusset Strengthening on the two top corners of some shipping containers, such as some insulated and refrigerated containers. It is achieved by having the top and side frames meet at an angle across the corner, rather than being squared off. Because of this, there is a loss of clearance at the top corners when loading the container.

Double hull System in tankers whereby an inner hull serves as a protection against oil spills in the event of the ship running aground or coming into contact with another ship or solid object. Sometimes referred to as a double skin. This system is an international requirement for various sizes and ages of vessel.

Double purchase Method of rigging a derrick using two double blocks, the lower one carrying the hook and having the rope or wire in four parts. The gain in power, known as purchase, is roughly equivalent to the number of parts of the rope, in this case by a factor of four. The Safe Working Load (SWL) of the derrick should not be exceeded in spite of the gain in power.

Double sling Attachment to a crane consisting of two lengths of chain joined at one end to a single ring. At the other end, each has a cargo hook. The chains are placed around the load and hooked onto the chain or ring.

Double-bottom (tank) Space between the floor of a ship's holds and the bottom of the ship. Its purpose is to help prevent seawater entering the ship in the event of running aground. It is used for the carriage of fuel oil or fresh water or, if the ship is not carrying a cargo, for water ballast.

Double-rigged Said of a hatchway which is served by two derricks.

Down by the head Said of a ship whose draught forward is slightly deeper than her draught aft. This often makes the handling of the ship difficult at sea. Also referred to as trimmed by the head. When a ship's draught aft is slightly deeper than its draught forward, it is said to be **down by the stern** or trimmed by the stern.

Down to its marks Said of a ship whose hull is immersed to the appropriate load line and which cannot therefore load any further cargo. *See also* **Load line**.

Draught Depth to which a ship is immersed in the water; this depth varies according to the design of the ship and will be greater or lesser depending not only on the weight of the ship and everything on board, such as cargo, ballast, fuel and spares, but also on the density of the water in which the ship is lying. A ship's draught is determined by reading its draught marks, a scale marked on the ship's stem and stern. The term 'draught' is also commonly used to describe the depth of water at a port or place. Also spelled **draft**.

Dredger Vessel designed to remove mud or sand from the sea bed or from a river bed. This is often done at or near a port to increase the depth of water or to restore it to its previous depth. This enables access to a port by vessels with deeper draught or allows a ship to carry a greater weight of cargo. The methods of dredging are by suction, buckets and grab. The suction method uses a pipe and a submersible pump to suck sand. The bucket method uses a continuous supply of buckets which reach to the sea bed and scrape up the sand or aggregate. A grab may also be employed on the end of a crane. All three operations transfer the sand or aggregate into the hold or into hoppers and thence to barges for removal. In some cases, the ship's hold may have a bottom opening through which the sand is dropped out at sea. Dredgers are sometimes referred to as sand dredgers or sand carriers.

Drum handler Lift truck designed to carry large drums, such as oil drums, either one or two at a time. These are held in position by clamps which are lowered onto the upper surface of the drums.

Dry cargo container or **dry freight container** or **dry van container** Also known as a general purpose container, this is the most widely used shipping container. Used mainly for general cargo, it is typically made from steel, is fully enclosed and is loaded and discharged through a set of full-height rear doors. The floor is covered with timber planking or plywood sheeting and cargo is secured to lashing points normally along the sides at floor level. The

Dry dock

dry freight container is made in several standard sizes, the commonest of which are 20 feet and 40 feet long. *See Figs. **40**, 67b.*

Fig. 40 Dry van container; this one is a 20-footer

Dry dock Enclosed basin from which all the water is pumped out to enable ships to be surveyed and repaired while out of the water. Ships offered for sale are normally inspected in a dry dock by prospective purchasers. Also referred to as a graving dock.

Duct keel Tunnel that accommodates pipelines and which runs longitudinally along the centre line of a ship under the inner plating.

Dumb Said of a craft which does not possess its own motive power or its own means of control. It requires to be towed or pushed. Such a craft is unmanned but has greater usable cargo space. An example is a **dumb barge**.

Dunnage Materials of various types, often timber or matting, placed among cargo for separation, and hence protection from damage, for ventilation and, in the case of certain cargoes, to provide a space in which the forks of a forklift truck may be inserted. Dunnage is used in the holds of a ship and also in shipping containers.

Dunnage bag *See* **Air bag**.

E-seal   *See* **Electronic seal**.

Edge protector   Packaging accessory, in a number of designs aimed at various products, which is intended to protect the edges of a product while being transported or in a warehouse. Edges and corners are the most vulnerable parts of a product or packaging. *See Fig. 41.*

Fig. 41 Edge protector

Edible oil carrier   Type of tanker used to carry different types of oil destined for human consumption. Because many of these oils solidify when cool, heating coils are required in the cargo tanks to maintain the correct temperature. High standards of cleanliness must be achieved including the cleaning of the pumps used for discharging.

Electronic seal   Seal fitted to a shipping container which is read by an electronic reader, containing details of the container and contents. It can show when and where any tampering has taken place and assist with clearance of containers at terminals. Often, a conventional seal is fitted with a radio tag which transmits data using radio frequency identification (RFID). Known as an e-seal or smart seal.

Elephant legs   Platforms onto which cargo is placed to enable a hydraulic trailer to be positioned underneath. *See Figs. 42, 59.*

Elevator

Fig. 42 Elephant legs

Elevator Equipment used to discharge some bulk cargoes such as grain by removing it from the hold using a continuous line of buckets or by suction and carrying it on a conveyor belt to store.

Empty container handler Name given to any truck dedicated to handling empty containers in a port or terminal. Commonly it is a frontlift truck which has a capacity much lower than a truck designed to lift loaded containers. It is generally capable of stacking containers three or four high and some models can stack six high. *See Fig. 43*.

Fig. 43 Empty container handler

Extension forks

End frame Structure at each end of a shipping container consisting of the end cross-members of the sides, base and roof together with the corner castings. It is normally constructed of steel.

End wall Part of a shipping container situated at the rear, that is, the end opposite the door of the container. It consists simply of the structure, made normally of steel or aluminium, surrounded by a steel frame.

Entrepot Place where goods are imported and subsequently re-exported. Often this is in a free-trade zone or Foreign-Trade Zone (FTZ) where goods which are imported and re-exported do not have to pay duties.

Euro container *See* **Palletwide container**.

Europallet European standard size pallet measuring 0.8 by 1.2 metres. It was designed principally for road and rail transport, although recent modifications to containers (*see* **Cellular palletwide container**) have allowed shipment of these pallets in cellular containerships.

Even keel Said of a ship whose draught forward is the same as her draught aft.

Explosimeter Instrument used to detect the presence of flammable gases in the tanks of a tanker.

Extension forks Forks, longer than the normal ones, fitted to a fork-lift truck in order to handle awkward loads or to obtain a greater reach. *See Fig. 44.*

Fig. 44 Extension forks

57

Extreme breadth   Maximum breadth of a ship measured from the outsides of her plating.

Fairlead   Fitting in the deck of a ship which guides the ropes when the ship is being moored.

Fairway navigable channel.   This can be at the entrance to a port or on a river. Sometimes termed a **fairway channel.**

Fall   Rope or wire used by lifting tackle.

Feeder   Wooden box, open at the bottom, which is built under the hatchway of a ship when grain in bulk is to be carried. The grain is loaded into the cargo compartment filling the feeder. This feeds the hold with grain as the cargo settles during the voyage, in order to prevent it from shifting.

Fender   Object used to keep a vessel away from, for example, a quay wall. Certain vessels are equipped with fenders at intervals along their length. These fenders may be of any material which is capable of absorbing shocks and thus protecting the vessel's plating; these would include rope, wood and pneumatic tyres. Quay walls may themselves have fenders.

Ferry   Vessel designed to provide sea transport, without sleeping accommodation, for passengers and sometimes vehicles, usually over a short sea crossing. Ferries carrying passengers and vehicles and also providing sleeping accommodation are termed passenger/vehicle/car ferries. These may carry cars and/or commercial vehicles together with their drivers. Ro-ro/vehicle/passenger ferries or simply ro-ro/passenger ferries carry unaccompanied ro-ro cargo on trailers as well as passengers and accompanied commercial vehicles. Vehicles and trailers are driven or towed on and off the ships on ramps and spend the voyage on special decks, normally segregated according to the type of vehicle.

Ferry port   Port that specialises in handling ferry services. It consists of a large paved area in which vehicles (cars, lorries and coaches) can park in readiness for driving onto the ferries, and berths normally equipped with ramps over which vehicles drive on and off the vessels.

Fertiliser   Type of bulk cargo shipped in very large quantities annually, used to provide nutrients for the soil to help crops grow. Common fertilisers are phosphate and potash. Phosphate is a salt mined from phosphate rock; potash is a salt derived from evaporated seawater. Urea is an organic compound, or a synthesised version thereof, widely used as a nitrogen fertiliser, and shipped

Fertiliser handling

in large quantities worldwide. It is transported in granular form. It may also be carried in bags in general purpose containers. *See* **Fertiliser handling** *and* **Fertiliser terminal**. *See Figs. 10a, 12.*

Fertiliser handling   Fertiliser is shipped in bulk and in bags. Large quantities of either may be shipped in bulk carriers; smaller quantities are carried in bulk containers when loose and in general purpose containers when in bags. Loading of bulk carriers is normally by conveyor leading to a spout. Discharge from the ship is normally by crane equipped with a grab. Discharge port terminals may have bagging facilities. See figs. **45a, 45b.**

Fig. 45a Portland, Oregon, USA, Terminal 5 potash export facility which handles about 2 million tons of potassium-based fertiliser each year

Fig. 45b Fertiliser in bulk being loaded via a mobile hopper to a truck

Fertiliser terminal

Fertiliser terminal Terminal in a port dedicated to handling fertiliser, such as potash. This is carried by ship in bags and in bulk. Bulk cargo is discharged by grab cranes and stored in silos. Bagged fertiliser is often on pallets which are discharged by crane, then moved by a fork-lift truck. Facilities for bulk cargoes include bagging equipment.

Fixed end flatrack Flatrack whose ends are not collapsible. Since it cannot make use of the space-saving capability of a collapsible flatrack, it is most suited to a trade in which it is unlikely to be empty.

Flat or **flatrack** Type of shipping container that has no sides or top. This is designed to accommodate in containerships cargoes, such as machinery, vehicles or forestry products, whose overall dimensions exceed those of a general purpose container. The flatrack is made up of a flat bed and two upright ends. These ends may be fixed or collapsible, or may simply fold flat, depending on the type of flatrack. The advantage of the latter two is that several flats may be stacked one on another when not carrying cargo, thus greatly reducing the volume which they would occupy in the ship. *See Figs. 27a, 27b, 46, 84, 134b.*

Fig. 46 A 20-foot collapsible flatrack

Flat bed trailer Road trailer with a flat bed. There are variations in length and types, including dropside trailers, tilt (or tipping) trailers and extendible trailers which can be lengthened or shortened according to the length of the cargo.

Flexible intermediate bulk carrier *See* **Intermediate bulk container (IBC).**

Flight of locks Series of locks placed near each other to convey ships to a much higher or lower level in gradual steps.

Floating crane Floating platform on which a crane is mounted. It is capable of being moved to any part of a port where it is needed, either alongside a berth or to an anchorage where it might be used for transhipment of cargo. Floating cranes often have the capacity to lift exceptionally heavy loads.

Floating dock Floating structure used for repairing ships out of the water. It is capable of being partially submerged to enable the ships to enter and leave.

Floating production, storage and offloading (FPSO) vessel or **Floating production, storage and offloading unit** Vessel used principally in the offshore oil industry and, to a lesser extent, gas. Oil flows to the unit where it is processed before being transferred by hose to a shuttle tanker for delivery ashore.

Flush deck ship Type of ship whose upper deck extends along her entire length, with no interruptions or well decks.

Flush hatch or **flush tween hatch cover** Hatch cover, in a tween deck vessel, which is flush with the deck to enable vehicles and fork-lift trucks to move easily across it.

Folding coil carrier Type of folding flatrack having a longitudinal well into which steel coils are lowered. This arrangement requires minimal securing as the well largely prevents movement of the coil.

Folding flat-flush deck Shipping container, similar to a folding flatrack, having either panelled ends or corner posts. The difference is that the ends or posts, when folded down, are flush with the bed of the container. The whole unit has a lower height, therefore, when folded and not in use.

Folding flatrack Shipping container, consisting of a flat bed and solid ends but with open sides, designed to carry cargoes of awkward size. When these flatracks are empty, the ends are folded down and several flatracks may then be interlocked in a stack that has the same dimensions as a single standard

Folding hatch cover

container, enabling them to be transported in the same way. Also called a collapsible flatrack.

Folding hatch cover Type of hatch cover which consists of several panels hinged together. These fold together when access to the hold is required. In some designs the panels are all stowed at one end of the hatchway while in others they are stowed at both ends. The operation of opening and closing these hatch covers is normally carried out hydraulically. Folding hatch covers are found on the weather deck and on the tween deck. *See Fig. 47.*

Fig. 47 Folding hatch covers

Force ice (to) To use the weight of a ship to penetrate ice. Charter-parties often contain a clause stipulating that the ship shall not be used by the charterer to force ice.

Forced ventilation System of ventilating the holds of a ship whereby ventilators on deck are closed off and air is circulated mechanically through the holds, being dried, if necessary, by dehumidifying equipment. This method of ventilating is useful when the outside air contains a high level of humidity, which would cause condensation damage to the cargo if introduced into the holds. This system is also known as mechanical ventilation.

Fore and aft stowage   Stowage along the length of a ship as opposed to stowage athwartships.

Fore peak tank   Small tank situated at the extreme forward end of a ship. It normally holds water ballast and is used in this way to assist in the trim of the ship, that is, the relationship of the draught forward to the draught aft.

Forecastle   Raised part of the forward end of a ship's hull.

Forest products carrier   Name given to any ship designed to carry forest products. These can be shipped in the form of logs, paper reels, pieces of timber or woodchips, with the design of the ship varying according to the type of product carried. Logs are normally carried in very basic, cheap ships as the cargo can cause damage. These ships need a high cubic capacity. Paper reels are either palletised and loaded using pallet elevators through side doors or stowed in specialised bulk carriers with box-shaped holds and a gantry crane (these carry cargoes of timber in planks as well), or, increasingly, secured on trailers and shipped on ro-ro ships. Ships carrying timber products are also sometimes referred to as timber carriers.

Forest products terminal   This type of dedicated terminal has different facilities for off-loading, storage and handling according to the type of product. Forest products come mainly in the form of panels (such as chipboard, plywood, fibreboard and veneers), paper reels, cut paper on pallets, packaged timber, logs and bales of pulp. Some packaged timber may be stored in the open but other products are generally sensitive to the weather and must be kept covered, in some cases in humidity-controlled storage. Handling is performed by fork-lift trucks with various attachments such as paper clamps or forks, depending on the product.

Fork   Horizontal prong, of which two are fitted to a fork-lift truck. These penetrate special pockets in shipping containers or the underside of pallets or between goods separated by dunnage, for the purpose of lifting. The forks are power driven and can be raised and lowered as required.

Fork-lift attachment   Device attached to a fork-lift truck, replacing the forks, to assist with lifting and moving specific cargoes. There are various types designed for different-shaped products or packaging. *See* **Barrel handler, Carton clamps, Container stripping boom, Paper clamp, Sidelift truck** *and* **Toplift**. *See Figs. 48a, 48b, 90b, 126b.*

Fork-lift attachment

Fig. 48a Fork-lift attachment for steel coils

Fig. 48b These pipes, or booms, are attached to fork-lift trucks and inserted into the bore or eye of steel coils to lift them

Fork-lift truck

Fork-lift pockets Openings in, for example, a shipping container or a pallet into which the forks of a fork-lift truck can be inserted for lifting purposes.

Fork-lift truck Vehicle used to move goods around a port or warehouse or within a ship. It is fitted with two horizontal prongs, known as forks, which are inserted into special openings in shipping containers or the underside of pallets or between goods separated by dunnage. The forks are power-driven and can be raised or lowered as required so that the goods may be lifted and positioned. As an alternative to forks, fork-lift trucks are often fitted with so-called fork-lift attachments of various types for dedicated purposes, such as lifting steel coils. *See also* **Fork-lift attachment**. *See Figs. 39, 49a, 49b, 49c, 125.*

Fig. 49a Fork-lift truck

Fig. 49b Fork-lift truck equipped with attachment for lifting steel coils. This model has a 32-tonne capacity

Forty-foot equivalent unit (FEU)

Fig. 49c Fork-lift truck equipped with low mast to enable it to be driven into shipping containers

Forty-foot equivalent unit (FEU)   Unit of measurement equivalent to one 40-foot shipping container. Thus, two 20-foot containers comprise an FEU. This measurement is used to quantify, for example, the container capacity of a ship, the number of containers carried on a particular voyage or over a period of time, or it may be the unit on which freight charges are based.

Forward   At or towards the stem or front of a ship.

Four-way pallet   Type of pallet in which the apertures intended to take the forks of a fork-lift truck are situated on all four edges. *See also* **Pallet, One-way pallet** *and* **Two-way pallet.**

Frame   One of a series of bars, often bulb flats, attached to the keel of a ship and supporting the plating at the sides of the ship. Because the frames cause loss of space in the holds for stowing some cargoes, ships have two capacities that are particularly important when contemplating bulk cargoes: the grain capacity, or simply the grain, used for free-flowing cargoes capable of filling the spaces between the frames, and the bale capacity, or bale, for cargoes which are not.

Free flow system   System employed in large tankers carrying one grade of cargo only, whereby oil flows from one compartment to another through sluice gates, rather than having complex pipelines.

Freeboard   Distance between the deck line, that is, the line representing the uppermost continuous deck, and the relevant load line, painted on the side of a ship. Freeboards are assigned by a government department or, if authorised by that department, a classification society.

Fresh water allowance (FWA)   Extra draught allowed by the load line regulations for loading in fresh water. This is because a ship's draught will be reduced when reaching the open sea where the density of water is greater.

Fresh water freeboard   Distance between the deck line of a ship and its fresh water load line.

Fresh water load line   Line painted on the sides of a ship which shows the maximum depth to which a ship's hull may be immersed when in fresh water. The line is marked F.

Fresh water timber freeboard   Distance between the deck line of a ship and its fresh water timber load line.

Fresh water timber load line   Line painted on the sides of a ship which shows the maximum depth to which the ship's hull may be immersed when in fresh water with a deck cargo of timber. The line is marked LF.

Fruit   Produce carried in large quantities around the world, including citrus fruit, deciduous fruit (such as apples and pears) as well as potatoes, bananas, grapes and other perishable produce. Fruit is carried in refrigerated ships and in refrigerated containers. *See* **Fruit and vegetable terminal**, **Fruit carrier**, **Fruit container**, **Refrigerated container** *and* **Refrigerated ship**.

Fruit and vegetable terminal   Terminal in a port dedicated to the handling and storage of fruit and vegetables. These include citrus fruit, deciduous fruit (such as apples and pears) as well as potatoes, bananas, grapes and other perishable produce. Cargo typically arrives in bags or cartons on refrigerated ships and can be discharged by various types of crane. Intermediate operations such as palletisation may be carried out and goods are stored in insulated sheds and temperature-controlled storage.

Fruit carrier   Ship equipped with a refrigerating system for carrying perishable goods, such as fruit, vegetables, meat and fish. Basic constructional features are similar to those of a general cargo ship. Refrigeration of cargo spaces is effected by circulating cool air at temperatures appropriate to the particular cargo. The cargo spaces are insulated, normally with aluminium or galvanised steel, to assist in maintaining the desired temperature. It is called a fruit carrier when dedicated to the fruit trade; otherwise it is termed a refrigerated ship or reefer ship.

Fruit container

Fig. 50 Travelling gantry crane

Fruit container   Insulated shipping container used for the carriage of fresh fruit. It has the same basic characteristics as those of a standard insulated container but has large internal dimensions to accommodate particular sizes of pallets and cases of fruit.

Fruit juice terminal   Terminal in a port dedicated to the handling and storage of fruit juice. This is generally carried in drums. These are stored in refrigerated chambers prior to distribution. A recent development is to carry fruit juice in large containers or tanks, stacked in the ship in a similar way to general purpose shipping containers. Fruit juice is carried in either a chilled or frozen state.

Full and down   Said of a ship whose holds are full of cargo and whose hull is immersed as far as the permitted load line. Such a condition is the ideal one for a ship operator as it maximises the use of the ship's cubic capacity and its permitted draught.

Gantry crane   Shore crane, with a wide span, used for marshalling and for stacking. Such cranes operate by straddling several rows of containers, placing and picking up containers as necessary. They can be either rail-mounted or rubber-tyred. Gantry cranes are also fitted to certain ships, such as some self-sustaining containerships. There is also a facility to tilt and angle containers when loading onto and off road vehicles. This type of crane is also known both as a travelling gantry crane and a bridge crane since it is in the form of a bridge. *See Figs. 50, 102, 110.*

Garage deck   Deck on a ro-ro vessel which accommodates cars.

General arrangement plan

Gas detection equipment   Equipment designed to detect noxious gases or a shortage of oxygen, either of which could be a hazard to entering a cargo space or other space on board a ship. Generally, the provision of such equipment is a legal requirement, for example in the United Kingdom, the Merchant Shipping (Carriage of Cargoes) Regulations 1999.

Gas terminal   Terminal in a port dedicated to the handling and storage of gases such as butane and propane. These products are kept in a liquid state in pressurised tanks at low temperatures. In some cases, storage takes the form of underground caverns.

Geared ship   Ship which is equipped with her own crane(s) or derrick(s). Such a ship is required for a voyage or trade where the loading or discharging port does not have shore cranes or where shore cranes are of insufficient lifting capacity or inefficient. A ship without her own lifting equipment is said to be **gearless**. *See Figs. 38, 51, 138.*

Fig. 51 Geared ship

General arrangement plan   Plan of a ship which shows the general layout: the number and positions of holds, hatches, tanks, cranes or derricks, decks and the location of the engine room and accommodation space. The general arrangement plan is of particular interest to a prospective charterer (such as a shipping line when supplementing its fleet) in determining the suitability of the ship for the intended voyage or trade.

General cargo Cargo consisting of goods shipped unpacked or packed, for example in cartons, crates, bags or bales, but specifically not cargo shipped in bulk, on trailers or in shipping containers. **A general cargo ship** is one designed to carry such cargo, often having several decks because of the number of ports served and the range of products carried.

General purpose container Also known as a dry freight container, this is the most widely used shipping container. Used mainly for general cargo, it is typically made from steel, is fully enclosed and is loaded and discharged through a set of full-height rear doors. The floor is normally covered with timber planking or plywood sheeting and cargo is secured to lashing points normally along the sides at floor level. The general purpose container is made in several standard sizes, the commonest of which are 20 feet and 40 feet long.

Generator set Power supply unit for a refrigerated container. It is either attached to a container when it is on a truck or train, such as a clip-on unit, or may be a separate container itself, into which a number of refrigerated containers are plugged when on a train.

Gin Type of large pulley with sheave and steel block found on a derrick.

Glass Glass is an example of a recyclable material. It may be recycled from used bottles and other glassware by crushing. It is transported in bulk by road, often by lorries with tipper trailers, and may be exported overseas, to manufacturing plants for use in the manufacture of new glassware. Handling in the port is normally by means of diggers, and loading and discharging of ships is by grabs. Crushed glass can be stored in the open at the port. *See Fig. 52*.

Fig. 52 Glass

GM Metacentric height, that is, the distance between the centre of gravity of a ship (G) and her metacentre (M). *See also* **Metacentric height**.

Gondola or **gondola flat** Flatrack of a type having open-framed ends and sides.

Gooseneck Steel piece inserted into an aperture in the front of a roll trailer or cassette trailer. The purpose is to raise the front end of the trailer, which is wheelless, off the ground for the purpose of towing by a tractor or pushing by a fork-lift truck. A gooseneck may be fixed or detachable.

Grab Device attached to a crane for unloading various types of bulk cargo, consisting of two or more parts that are brought together to 'grab' the cargo in the ship's hold and lift it out to transfer it to trucks, rail wagons or barges. Grabs with two parts or buckets which are brought together to lift cargo are sometimes called clam-shell grabs. Those with more than two parts are often called orange peel grabs or orange peel grapples. Grabs are operated in three different ways: mechanical (rope-type), hydraulic and diesel-hydraulic, depending on the source of power. *See Figs. 53a, 53b, 53c, 53d, 63.*

Fig. 53a Clamshell grab, used for many types of bulk cargoes

Grab

Fig. 53b Scissors grab, higher capacity grab used for a variety of bulk cargoes

Fig. 53c Cactus grab, used for scrap, biomass and other shredded materials

Grain handling

Fig. 53d Trimming grab, used to remove residual loads of different types of ore. It can handle large quantities by its ability to be opened to a wide radius

Grab crane or **grabbing crane** Type of crane equipped with a grab, a mechanical device that is lowered into a ship to grab or grip the cargo. It is used to discharge bulk cargoes such as coal, ore or phosphates from the ship's hold into hoppers and thence to conveyor belts leading to stockpiles or vehicle loading bays.

Grab type ship unloader Most usual type of discontinuous unloader, that is to say not automated. It is a dedicated dockside apparatus used to unload coal, ores, phosphates and other minerals. It consists of a grab hung from a wire under a crane. Performance is measured in tonnes per hour (TPH). *Also spelled* **grab-type ship unloader**. *See* **Unloader**.

Grain (1) Commodity shipped in bulk in large quantities around the world. It encompasses a number of cereal products, the main ones being wheat, barley, oil seed rape, oats, rye, sorghum and soya beans. Most are for human consumption, some for animal feed and, more recently, some for fuel for making electricity. *See* **Grain handling** *and* **Grain silo**.

Grain (2) or **grain capacity** Total cubic capacity of a ship's holds available for the carriage of grain or any other free-flowing bulk cargo that is capable of filling the space between the ship's frames. It is expressed in cubic feet or cubic metres. (Where a cargo is solid and not therefore capable of filling the spaces between the ship's frames, the corresponding capacity is known as the bale or bale capacity.)

Grain handling Grain is carried from farms by train and by lorries of various types. It is normally loaded into hopper wagons for transport by rail,

Grain handling

and bulk tipper lorries or tipper trailers or bulk road tankers, when carried by road. The name 'tipper' comes from its ability to tip at destination in order to discharge its contents. Road tankers are discharged either by tipping or by pneumatic suction. Such tankers are used for other dry bulk cargoes. Relatively small quantities are shipped in containers. At the load port, grain is stored in large silos, then fed along a conveyor, the end of which is positioned over the holds of the ship where it is dropped or fed with a spout into the ship. At the discharge port, it is unloaded by grab or suction. The biggest issue with the transport of grain is the threat of insect infestation, for which treatment is required. *See Figs.* **54a**, **54b**, **54c**, *96*.

Fig. 54a Bulk carrier loading grain stored in a dome-shaped silo via a conveyor and spout

Fig. 54b Port of Portland's Terminal 5 in Oregon, USA, one of the world's largest wheat export facilities. Each year about 3 million tons of grain pass through Terminal 5. Note wheat being loaded from a spout, and the ship's side-rolling hatch covers

Granite handling

Fig. 54c Loading grain using a spout

Grain silo Building used for the stowage of grain. It is often to be found at grain terminals where ocean vessels load and discharge. Silos are towers, tall and cylindrical in shape. *See Fig. 54a.*

Granite Rock used as a building material. It has many applications inside and outside: for interior use, it is often cut into tiles or worktops; for exterior applications it is cut into blocks and used for construction. It also has such diverse uses as kerbstones and monuments. *See* **Granite handling**.

Granite handling Granite is shipped in blocks normally of 5–30 tonnes but can be as much as 50 tonnes. At the quarry, fork-lift trucks are used to move the blocks. At the port, granite is stored outside as it is not necessary to protect it from the elements; chains are normally slung round the blocks for lifting into and out of the ship. In large quantities, granite is carried conventionally in the holds of bulk carriers. Smaller quantities are shipped in closed containers, provided they do not exceed permitted weights and are well secured. *See Fig. 55.*

Grapple

Fig. 55 Granite blocks

Grapple Attachment to a crane which consists of a pair of large pincers at the end of a wire. These grip the topmost logs of a strapped bundle for the purpose of lifting. Also known as a log grapple.

Graving dock Enclosed basin from which all the water is pumped out to enable ships to be surveyed and repaired while out of the water. Ships offered for sale are normally inspected in a graving dock by prospective purchasers. Also referred to as a dry dock.

Great circle route Shortest route between two points.

Gross tonnage (GT) Figure representing the total of all the enclosed spaces within a ship, arrived at by means of a formula that has as its basis the volume measured in cubic metres. The gross tonnage has replaced the gross register tonnage.

Guillotine door Door found at the stern of some ro-ro ships which is raised when open and lowered when in the closed position, resembling in its configuration the instrument of execution from which it gets its name. It is found on ships which have no ramp fitted and which therefore require a shore-based linkspan. Accordingly, it provides a watertight barrier against the entry of seawater. *See Fig. 56.*

Half-height container

Fig. 56 Guillotine door

Gun tackle Method of rigging a derrick using two blocks, the upper one fixed and the lower one carrying the hook, with the rope or wire in two parts at the lower block. The gain in power is roughly equivalent to the number of parts of the rope at the lower block. In this case, the pull is doubled. This gain is termed the purchase. The safe working load of the derrick should nevertheless not be exceeded.

Gunny bag Bag or sack made of coarse fibre widely used for the carriage of certain bulk cargoes such as sugar.

Gunny matting Coarse fibre matting, one of the many types of material used as dunnage in ships, mainly for the separation and protection of cargoes.

Guy Wire or rope fitted on either side of a ship's derrick and used to control the moving of the derrick into the desired position. Often the guy is fed through a block at the top of which is a single strand, known as a **guy pennant**, which leads to the derrick head.

Half-height container Open-top shipping container which has a standard length and width but only 4 feet 3 inches (about 1.3 metres) high, half the standard height. It is suitable for the carriage of dense cargoes, such as scrap

Hand hook

metal, steel bars or pipes and stone, as these take up relatively little space in relation to their weight. The half-height container is also suitable for loading and discharging in premises with insufficient height to take a full-height container. Two **half-heights** (as they are often called) occupy one cell in a containership. As with the full-height open-top, the half-height is covered by a waterproof tarpaulin.

Hand hook   Curved piece of steel with a point, held in the hand by a docker, used to attach to sacks of cargo for the purpose of moving them from place to place, both on shore and in the hold of a ship. Also known as a stevedore's hook or docker's hook (as distinct from a cargo hook which is attached to a crane or derrick).

Hand pallet truck   Small truck used to move loaded pallets, pulled along by hand. The forks are positioned in the pockets of the pallet, then the handle is pumped to raise the pallet off the ground sufficiently to wheel it along. To lower the pallet, a trigger grip is squeezed by the operator and the forks are lowered hydraulically. Hand pallet trucks come with different lifting capacities, often 1 tonne but which may be 2.5 tonnes or more. Also known as a pump truck, they can be mechanical or have an electric motor. *See Fig. 57.*

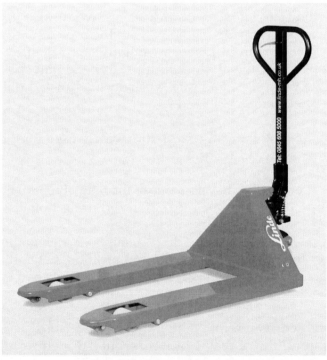

Fig. 57 Hand pallet truck

Handymax Bulk carrier of about 25,000 tonnes deadweight, so called because it is suitable for many different trades.

Handy-sized bulker Bulk carrier at the smaller end of the range of sizes associated with this type of ship, typically up to 30,000–35,000 tonnes deadweight. Within this category are ships which are intended to trade into the Great Lakes of North America; their dimensions are within the constraints of the St Lawrence Seaway, which is the limiting factor in this trade.

Harbour A natural or artificial shelter for ships.

Hardtop container Shipping container having the same dimensions as a general purpose 20-foot or 40-foot container but which has a removable hard top. The roof may be lifted off by a fork-lift truck. This makes it suitable for heavy loads which are easier to load from the top by means of a crane.

Hatch or **hatchway** or **hatch opening** Opening in the deck of a ship through which cargo is loaded into, and discharged from, the hold. It is closed off by means of a hatch cover which may be of various kinds. The number of hatches may correspond exactly to the number of holds, although a ship may have two hatches serving one hold, dividing the hold either along its length or its width. Loading hatches and discharge hatches are to be found in bulk containers: loading hatches are openings in the roof of the container through which the cargo is loaded by gravity; discharge hatches are openings in the rear door or front end of the container through which the cargo is unloaded when the container is tipped.

Hatch beam One of a set of steel sections stretching along the length of a hatchway onto which boards, known as hatch boards, are placed to close the hatchway. This arrangement is used on older vessels and has largely been replaced by steel hatch covers. The beams onto which the ends of the hatch boards rest are known as king beams while those which support the centres are called sister beams.

Hatch coaming Steel surround to a hatchway which rises vertically from the deck of a ship. Its functions are to prevent water washing into the hold and to lessen the risk of any person who may be working on the deck falling through the open hatchway. Also known simply as the coaming.

Hatch cover Means of closing the hatchway of a ship. There are various types, for example wooden boards laid across the hatchway or steel sections that roll to one side or to one end. They are designed to be watertight so as to keep out rain and seas breaking over the ship. Hatch covers may be on the weather deck and on the tween deck. Also known as a hatch. It is important to

Hatch cover ramp

know the strength of the hatch cover, especially when loading dense cargoes. This is expressed in tonnes per square metre and represents the maximum weight which can be loaded onto it. This limitation is calculated by the ship's classification society. *See also* **Folding hatch cover, Lift-away hatch cover, Piggyback hatch cover, Rolling hatch cover, Sliding** *and* **Stacking hatch cover.** *See Figs. 47, 58, 68, 122, 129.*

Fig. 58 Side-rolling hatch covers

Hatch cover ramp Type of internal ramp in a ro-ro ship, which forms part of the main deck and can provide a watertight deck closure.

Hatch opening or **hatchway.** *See* **Hatch.**

Hazardous materials or **hazardous goods.** *See* **Dangerous goods.**

Head (of a ship) Bows or forward part of a ship. A ship is said to be down by the head if its draught forward is deeper than its draught aft.

Head (of a shipping container) End of a container which is opposite the doors.

Header bar Cross-bar situated over the doors of an open-top shipping container, which forms part of the end frame. When loading or unloading is in

Heavy lift

progress, the header bar may be swung out of the way or completely removed, depending on the particular design.

Heating coil   System of steel tubing fitted in the tanks of a tanker which, by means of steam, maintains viscous cargoes, such as bitumen or heavy oil, in a liquid state and capable of being pumped out. The arrangement of the tubing is designed to give a heating surface at a rate measured in square feet to the ton of cargo or square metres to the tonne, the exact rate depending on the particular ship.

Heavy lift   Generally, a lift which requires special lifting equipment by virtue of its weight. When carried by a shipping line, a heavy lift may be described as any lift which exceeds a specific weight as stated in the line's tariff and which is normally the subject of a heavy lift additional. Examples of heavy lifts are generators, locomotives, pressure vessels, wind turbines and drilling rigs. *See also* **Floating crane, Heavy lift crane, Heavy lift derrick, Heavy lift ship, Jumbo derrick, Low loader, Samson-post, Shears** *and* **Spreader beam**. *See Figs.* **59, 143**.

Fig. 59 Heavy lift involving the use of a spreader to deal with a long and wide piece; note the elephant legs under the cargo

Heavy lift crane Crane designed to lift unusually heavy loads even up to several hundred tonnes in one lift. Often a ship may have only one such lift to undertake and a mobile crane is brought in specially while shore cranes or the ship's own lifting gear handle the other cargo. A heavy lift crane may be on tracks or floating. *See Fig. 60.*

Fig. 60 Heavy lift spreader in the foreground; it keeps two cranes apart while they lift a wide load in tandem

Heavy lift derrick Ship's derrick used for lifting unusually heavy loads. Traditionally capable of handling lifts up to, typically, 100 tonnes, modern heavy lift derricks are capable of lifting several hundred tonnes. Also known as jumbo derrick.

Heavy lift ship Ship designed to lift and carry exceptionally heavy loads such as railway locomotives. There are three basic methods of loading and discharging such cargoes: lift-on/lift-off by means of a heavy lift derrick fixed to the deck of the ship; float-in/float-out whereby the ship is partially submerged during loading and discharging; ro-ro whereby the cargo is wheeled on and off the ship.

High cube cellular palletwide container Cellular palletwide container which has a higher cubic capacity than the standard size and thus can carry a greater volume of cargo. The extra capacity is achieved either by increasing the height of the container to 9 feet 6 inches compared to the standard 8 feet. *See also* **Cellular palletwide container**. *See Fig. 61.*

Hoistable car deck

Fig. 61 High cube cellular palletwide container; this model has compressed bamboo flooring, a recent innovation

High cube (general purpose) container A 40-foot container which, at 9 feet 6 inches high, is taller than the normal container. It is suitable for light, voluminous cargoes or cargoes that would otherwise be overheight.

High cube reefer Variation of the refrigerated container that has a higher cubic capacity than the standard size reefer container and thus can carry a greater volume of cargo. The extra capacity is achieved either by increasing the height to 9 feet 6 inches compared to the standard 8 feet or by designing it so that the space taken by the clip-on diesel generator is over and above the standard dimensions of the container. *See also* **Refrigerated container**.

Hog (to) Said of a ship where the ends are depressed below the level of the centre. This bending of the ship's plating is caused by the effect of waves on the ship when at sea or by the uneven distribution of weight along her length. It may result in damage or distortion to the hull.

Hoistable car deck Deck on a ship on which vehicles are stowed when being carried between ports. This type of deck is stowed under the deckhead

Hold

when not being used and lowered on wires into its operational position. In some bulk carriers, hoistable decks are lowered from under the wing tanks and centre pontoons are lifted into position from their stowage position on deck.

Hold Space below the deck of a ship used to carry cargo. If a ship has more than one hold, they are numbered consecutively from one upwards starting with the forward most; this is done for the purposes of identifying the holds and locating the cargo stowed in them.

Hooded coil carrier Shipping container, consisting of a flat bed and a cover which is supported by a framework, used to carry steel coils. It has a well into which the coils are placed and may have a fixed end. The well largely prevents movement of the coils, which therefore require minimal securing.

Hook Piece of steel, often curved, fixed to the end of the rope of a crane or derrick, to which the ropes, slings or other lifting accessories placed around goods are attached for the purpose of lifting. Variations in the design exist, for example, to help prevent the hook snagging or catching on anything while it is being raised or to stop the load from slipping. Also known as a cargo hook. A spreader is sometimes used with a hook, when it is known as a **hook beam**. Also referred to as ship's hook particularly in the expression 'ex ship's hook', although this often denotes a location specified in the sales contract. *See Figs. 62, 93.*

Fig. 62 Type of hook

Hose test (to)

Hopper Container with a funnel at its base, or an angled construction, to permit feeding by gravity of a free-flowing substance such as grain into another container below. For example, it may be convenient to discharge sugar in bulk by means of a grab that deposits its load into a cistern-like hopper from which it is fed by gravity onto a horizontal conveyor. *See Figs. 24b, 45b, 63.*

Hopper barge or **hoppered barge** Barge used in dredging operations: mud and sand are transferred to it from a dredger and taken away to be discharged at sea through an opening in the bottom of the barge.

Hopper cars Rail wagons with hoppered or funnel-shaped bodies capable of discharging free-flowing cargoes through a funnel to a tip.

Fig. 63 Mobile hopper underneath a grab which is being used to load a free-flowing bulk cargo onto trucks

Hoppered holds Holds found in bulk carriers; these have the cut-away corners found in some hoppers behind which are hoppered or funnel-shaped tanks used for ballast or for stability when carrying certain cargoes.

Hose test (to) To test a hatch cover for watertightness by spraying water on it with a hose.

House flag

House flag Ship's flag bearing the emblem of the shipowner or shipping line. Some time charter-parties allow the charterers to fly their house flag during the period of the charter.

Hovercraft Fast-moving craft that travels along a few feet above the surface of the sea by means of a cushion of air forced downwards. These craft are designed to carry commercial vehicles as well as cars and foot passengers. Specialist hovercraft carry general cargo and containers over difficult terrain.

Ice-breaker Ship whose hull is specially strengthened to enable it to crush ice using its own weight in order to make a passage sufficient for other ships to navigate. *See Fig. 64.*

Fig. 64 Canadian ice-breaker 'Henry Larsen'; it is a medium gulf/river ice-breaker, but also provides search and rescue support during the summer season, escorting large ships in southern Canadian waters, as well as Arctic areas, and conducts limited oceanographic, meteorological and other scientific work in regions inaccessible to conventional ships. An air bubbler system, which also acts as a side thruster, is fitted and controlled from the wheelhouse to reduce hull friction during ice-breaking operations

Ice-breaking bulk carrier Bulk carrier suitably strengthened to enable it to navigate in conditions of ice, particularly in the ore trade carried on in the Canadian Arctic.

Ice-strengthened ship Ship whose hull is strengthened to enable it to navigate in ice conditions. The shell plating is thicker and the bows reinforced.

Indicative seal Type of seal on the doors of a shipping container intended to show, when damaged, that unauthorised access has been made to the container.

Inert gas system (IGS) System of preventing any explosion in the cargo tanks of a tanker by replacing the cargo as it is being pumped out by an inert gas, often the exhaust of the ship's engine.

Inflatable dunnage Inflated bag used to fill gaps between goods when stowed in rail wagons, trucks, shipping containers or in ships. They are a means of load bracing or cushioning, the purpose being to prevent the shifting of goods. In a container, for example, they are positioned across the length or width and then inflated to brace the load against the walls or ends of the container.

Inspection (of containers) Scrutiny of containers by the authorities to ensure that they do not contain unauthorised or illegal goods or stowaways. Scanning equipment is often used to view inside containers and trucks without the need to open them, thus saving time and avoiding the need to unpack boxes or cartons.

Insulated container Shipping container that is lined, normally with plywood, so as to minimise the effects of changes in temperature on the cargo and to reduce condensation. This container is suitable for perishable goods and other cargoes which require protection from temperature changes without the necessity of refrigeration. The inside dimensions of an insulated container are less than those of a general purpose container because of the lining. In trades where there is an imbalance in one direction of cargo requiring insulated containers, these may be used on the return leg to carry clean general cargo.

Integral reefer Refrigerated container whose refrigeration unit is built in, as distinct from the conair type, which is attached to a ventilation system on board ship. These are connected by means of reefer plugs to the ship's power supply.

Intelligent clamp Type of clamp truck fitted with a computer, designed to sense the optimum pressure needed to lift reels of paper so as to avoid slippage or squeezing.

Intermediate bulk container (IBC) Container used for the carriage of bulk products or liquids. Its use makes it possible to avoid using special equipment such as tank containers or bulk containers. Generally made from steel or plastic, it is reusable and designed to be stackable, thus making it a more efficient

Intermediate bulk carrier liner bag

transport option than a drum, for example. It may take the form of a steel frame into which a liner is placed to hold a liquid cargo. It may have openings in the base to take the forks of a fork-lift truck or may have these pockets built in. Also known as an **intermediate bulk carrier**.

Intermediate bulk carrier liner bag   Bag placed inside an intermediate bulk carrier to facilitate its reuse.

Intermodal loading unit   Container or swapbody capable of being carried on more than one mode of transport.

Internal ramp   Ramp inside a ro-ro ship that connects one deck with another. These are of two basic types: fixed and movable. Fixed ramps may be curved or straight. The curves at the top and bottom prevent the underside of the vehicles touching the ground. Movable ramps allow vehicles to be moved from one deck to a choice of decks as required. Stowing ramps can be secured in the elevated position to allow greater headroom for larger vehicles. Ramps can also provide a watertight deck closure when forming part of the main deck; these are known as hatch cover ramps.

Iron and steel terminal   Terminal in a port dedicated to the handling and storage of iron and steel products. These products are of many types having different handling and storage requirements. There are long products (such as 20-metre universal beams or 30-metre rails), products which are both long and wide (such as plates) and coils of different sizes and weights. Increasingly, steel is required to be kept in undercover storage before being shipped or distributed but some products may be left out in the open, particularly those requiring processing such as shotblasting and painting at destination. Terminals are normally equipped with cranes capable of lifting heavy pieces or bundles.

Iron ore   Largest dry bulk cargo shipped worldwide, used principally in the production of steel. The ore is crushed in order to make suitably sized lumps for steel furnaces. The smaller particles resulting from this process are known as fines. Further processing to reduce impurities results in concentrates. Sometimes after further processing, the ore is pelletised into uniform-size pieces suitable for the blast furnace. Iron ore is shipped in all these forms: lump, fines, concentrate and pellets. *See* **Iron ore handling**.

Iron ore handling   Iron ore is typically carried by train, normally in trainloads on a dedicated line, from the mine to the loading port. At the port, rail wagons are tipped one by one by a wagon tippler, otherwise known as a rotary dumper. This causes the ore to fall onto a conveyor which takes the cargo to a stacking area in readiness for loading. Loading is effected by conveyor tipping the cargo into the holds of the ship, or by spout (*see* **Shiploader**). In both cases, the equipment is directed into the appropriate location in the ship. The cargo may also be transhipped from a self-unloading barge, in other words, a barge which has its own conveyor system. Discharge is normally effected by grab (*see* **Grab**). *See also* **Ore carrier, Ore/bulk/oil carrier (OBO), Ore/oil carrier (OO)** *and* **Ore pellet carrier.**

Jetty Structure, often of masonry, projecting out to sea, designed to protect a port from the force of the waves but also used to berth ships.

Jib Arm of a crane that extends outwards and from which hangs, at one end, a hook, grab or magnet used for lifting goods.

Jib crane Type of crane equipped with a jib, that is, an arm that extends outwards and from which hangs a device, such as a hook, grab or magnet, for lifting cargo. A jib crane may be fixed, on wheels, on rails or on crawlers. It operates using three distinct motions: luffing, the lowering and raising of the jib until it reaches the point where the cargo is to be picked up or set down; hoisting, the lifting and lowering of the cargo; slewing, the rotating of the crane, for example from ship to quay. *See Fig. 65.*

Fig. 65 Rail-mounted jib cranes, Churchill Dock, Antwerp, Belgium

Jumbo derrick Name given to a ship's heavy lift derrick. This derrick is used for lifting unusually heavy loads. Traditionally capable of handling lifts up to, typically, 100 tonnes, modern heavy lift derricks are capable of lifting several hundred tonnes.

Jumboising Conversion of a ship to increase cargo-carrying capacity by dividing her and adding a new section.

Kaolin Kaolin, or china clay, is used in the production of paper, as well as in ceramics and a number of other products. It is normally shipped in a dry bulk state but may also be in bags, either small or bulk bags, or in the form of slurry. *See* **Kaolin handling** *and* **Kaolin terminal**.

Kaolin handling Kaolin in bulk is transported to the load port by train in bulk wagons. At the load and discharge ports, it may be stored in silos or covered warehouse. It is shipped in bulk carriers and sometimes smaller ships; occasionally, smaller quantities are carried in bulk containers. Loading of ships is effected by conveyor and discharged by suction or grabs, often with dust-extracting equipment. Processed kaolin, which may take the form of pellets, lump or powder, is normally packed into small bags of, say, 25 or 50 kgs, or bulk bags of, for example, 1 tonne. It is shipped in bulk carriers and smaller ships; smaller quantities are carried in bulk containers. When in slurry form, it is transported by road tanker, rail tank wagon, or may be pumped through a dedicated pipeline to the loading port. At the load and discharge ports, it is stored in large tanks and pumped to and from the tanker.

Kaolin terminal Terminal in a port dedicated to the handling and storage of kaolin, or china clay. Different qualities are stored separately in silos or covered warehouses, and distribution facilities often include bagging operations, or it may be converted to slurry at the load port prior to shipment. *See* **Kaolin handling**.

Keel Longitudinal girder at the lowest point of a ship from which the framework is built up.

Keel clearance Minimum distance between the bottom of a ship and the bed of a river or sea, required by some authorities as a safety margin because of unseen hazards or climatic changes in the depth of water. Also known as underkeel clearance.

King beam Steel section which stretches along the length of a hatchway onto which the ends of boards, known as hatch boards, are placed so as to close the hatchway. This arrangement is used on older vessels and has largely been replaced by steel hatch covers.

Laker Bulk carrier specially designed to trade in the North American Great Lakes system. Lakers are normally geared and possess an unusually large number of hatches. Some never leave the Lakes and indeed a few are too large to negotiate the St Lawrence Seaway's locks. Others trade worldwide to avoid being laid up in the Lakes during the winter. They are used to carry iron ore from St Lawrence and from ore terminals within the Lakes to steel mills in the US mid-West and grain from the western Lakes to St Lawrence. *See Figs. 24a, 66.*

Fig. 66 Cement carrier 'Alpena', one of the oldest ships trading in the Great Lakes

Lane metres (LM) Unit by means of which the decks on a ro-ro ship are measured. The number of lane metres which a ro-ro ship has is a way of describing the capacity of the ship, for example when comparing her with another ship. The total number of lane metres make up the total lane length.

Large gas carrier LPG carrier in the 52,000–60,000 cubic metre capacity class.

Lash (to) To hold goods in position by the use of, for example, wires, ropes, chains or straps. *See also* **Lashings**.

Lashing point Point on the deck of a ship, on a vehicle, a piece of cargo or inside a shipping container, to which wires, chains, ropes or straps are attached in order to hold goods in position. Normally, it consists of a metal loop. These are of various types and shapes, with different names such as lashing rings, lashing eyes or d-rings. *See Figs. 67a, 67b.*

Fig. 67a Power transformer on a 170-tonne (170 tonnes carrying capacity) roll trailer; the trailer is 26 feet long; note the large circular lifting points on the left face of the transformer, and the lashing points to which chains are attached

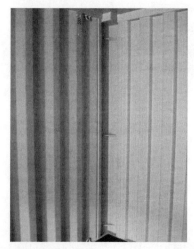

Fig. 67b Interior of a 20-foot dry van container; it shows two lashing rings: one at the top, the other near the floor, three (horizontal) lashing bars and a vent next to the top lashing ring

Lashings   Devices, often wires, chains, ropes or straps, used to secure a cargo on a ship, truck or rail wagon, or inside a shipping container. When carried on the deck of a ship, the containers themselves are lashed. The lashings are attached to fittings on or in the vehicle or on the ship and are often stretched tight by means of tensioners. The purpose of lashing cargo is to prevent it from moving during transit, which could result in loss or damage.

Latitude   Distance North or South of the Equator, expressed in degrees, minutes and seconds.

Lay-by berth   Part of a port where a ship which is awaiting a loading or discharging berth may moor.

Length between perpendiculars (LBP)   Length of a ship measured at a certain level between two perpendicular lines. The method of calculating this distance varies according to different classification societies but, typically, is from the foremost point of the ship to the aftermost point or to the after side of the rudder post, measured at the ship's summer load line.

Length overall (LOA)   The maximum length between the extreme ends, forward and aft, of a ship. This measurement is often required to determine, for example, whether a ship can negotiate a particular lock or whether she can be accommodated at a specific berth. Also referred to as the overall length.

Level luffing crane   Luffing crane which allows the load to remain level while the jib is luffed (lowered or raised).

Lift crane   Name given to a crane used with a hook to lift goods on and off ships by contrast with other methods of loading and discharging, namely, drag line, grab and magnet.

Lift truck satellite   Pallet truck which is attached to a fork-lift truck and operated from there by remote control. It goes into a shipping container for the purpose of loading, unloading and moving palletised goods while the fork-lift truck remains outside the container.

Lift-away hatch cover   Hatch cover consisting of a single slab, which is lifted off when access to the hold is required. It may be lifted by shore cranes or the ship's gear and stacked with others out of the way until the hatch is to be closed. This type of hatch cover is typically found on cellular containerships but is also fitted to multi-purpose and heavy-lift ships. This hatch cover is also termed a pontoon hatch cover. *See Fig. 68.*

Lift-on/lift-off

Fig. 68 Lift-away hatch covers

Lift-on/lift-off System of loading and discharging whereby cargo is lifted on and off a ship by the use of cranes. It is normally said of shipping containers.

Lifting point Point on a piece of machinery or other cargo to which lifting equipment is attached to enable the piece of cargo to be lifted. *See Fig. 67a*.

Light displacement Weight of a ship's hull, machinery, equipment and spares. This is often the basis on which ships are paid for when purchased for scrapping. The difference between the loaded displacement and the light displacement is the ship's deadweight.

Lighter Type of barge used to carry to a port part of a cargo of an ocean ship. This operation is carried out, for example, when the draught of a ship is too deep to reach the port, sufficient cargo being discharged to lighters to reduce the draught.

Limber board Removable board that is lifted to inspect a bilge.

Limestone Rock that has many uses, for example, as a building material, in glass-making and as a constituent of cement. It is transported in bulk in powder form, carried in bulk carriers, loaded by shiploader (conveyor) (*see* **Continuous ship loader**) directed over the holds and discharged by continuous ship unloader (*see* **Continuous (ship) unloader (CSU)**). *See Fig. 69.*

Fig. 69 Unloading limestone

Linkspan Surface which forms a shore-based interface with ships, enabling mainly vehicles to be driven on and off ships such as ro-ro ships, which have no ramps. It is specially constructed to meet geographical constraints in a port and the physical requirements such as the type of ship which will be using it. It may be fixed or floating depending on the particular site. As well as road vehicles, passengers and, less commonly, rail wagons use linkspans as a link between the ship and shore. Also spelled **link span**. *See Fig. 70.*

Fig. 70 Linkspan at the port of Immingham, UK, connecting a stern ramp to the shore

Liquefied natural gas carrier (LNG carrier)

Liquefied natural gas carrier (LNG carrier) or **liquid natural gas carrier** Vessel designed to carry liquefied natural gas (methane). The gas is held in a liquid state by pressure and refrigeration. The cargo-carrying capability consists of special tanks whose upper sections often protrude above the deck height in domed or cylindrical form. Also known as a methane carrier.

Liquefied petroleum gas carrier (LPG carrier) or **liquid petroleum gas carrier** Ship designed to carry liquefied petroleum gas, such as butane or propane. These are carried in special tanks under pressure and at very low temperatures. The tanks are often rectangular in section and may be flanked by wing or hopper tanks used to carry water ballast.

Livestock carrier Ship used for the carriage of livestock, mainly sheep. Many are converted from oil tankers and dry cargo ships, although a few have been purpose-built. Ships that have been converted have essentially only had livestock decks added; these consist of weather-protected pens in which the livestock are carried. Also known as a sheep carrier.

LNG Liquefied natural gas or liquid natural gas. *See* **Liquefied natural gas carrier (LNG carrier)**.

Load line One of the lines, 230 millimetres in length and 25 millimetres in width, painted on the sides of a ship, which show the maximum depths to which the ship may be immersed when arriving at, sailing through, or putting to sea in the different load line zones. The positioning of these lines is determined by the rules agreed at the International Conference on Load Lines, which have been ratified by many maritime countries. *See also* **Down to its marks**. Load lines are also marked on the walls of shipping containers and warehouses to show the maximum height to which goods may be stacked. Also spelled **loadline**.

Load line mark Ring painted on the sides of a ship amidships, bisected by a horizontal line that is level with the ship's summer load line.

Load line zone Geographical area, defined by the International Conference on Load Lines, where a ship's hull may be immersed no deeper than the appropriate load line. There are five types of zone: tropical, summer, winter, seasonal tropical and seasonal winter. The first three are permanent, that is, the one appropriate load line applies all year round. The last two being seasonal, the corresponding load lines apply at certain periods only, depending on the zone; for the rest of the year, the summer load line applies.

Lock

Loaded displacement or **load displacement**   Weight of a ship's hull, machinery, equipment, spares, cargo, bunkers, fresh water and crew when the ship is immersed to its summer load line. The difference between the loaded displacement and the light displacement is the ship's deadweight.

Loading hatch   Hatch opening found in the roof of a bulk container through which the cargo is loaded by gravity. Bulk containers normally have three such hatches. *See Fig. 71.*

Fig. 71 Interior of a bulk container in which three roof hatches can be seen, as well as the tipping hatch at the foot of the end wall

Locating cone   Device for positioning one shipping container on top of another using the corner castings. This is necessary on ships having no cell guides.

Lock   Space in a river or canal, or separating a dock from the sea, enclosed at the sides by walls and at each end by gates, into which ships and other craft enter in order to be floated up or down to a different level or to gain access to, or to leave, an enclosed dock. Ships enter a lock through one gate or pair of gates, which are then closed. Sufficient water is allowed in or out, as the case may be, either by opening sluice gates or valves where these are installed, or by opening the gates by a small amount to bring the level within the lock equal to the level on the other side of the lock. When this is achieved, sluices

Lock

or valves in the second lock gate, if these are installed, are opened, followed by the gates themselves, and the ship is able to leave. Alongside river locks are often weirs or dams which allow water to run downstream as required. *See Figs. 72a, 72b, 72c, 72d.*

Fig. 72 Lock. The illustration is of Iroquois Lock on the St. Lawrence Seaway. Fig. 72(a) shows the gates at one end closed. Fig. 72(b) shows the ship arrester in position in the foreground which is designed to stop a ship from hitting the lock gates if she is unable stop by herself.

Fig. 72 Lock (continued). Fig. 72(c) shows the lock gates open. Fig. 72(d) shows the other end of the lock with ship arrester in the foreground, curved lock gates immediately behind (these are curved to allow a current of up to 8 kph). In the background are a general purpose crane and a lift bridge in the open position, used to carry foot and motor traffic across the lock.

Log carrier

Log carrier Ship designed to carry whole cargoes of logs. Normally a bulk carrier with stanchions or uprights along each side to contain the cargo of logs. Because of the stowage factor of this commodity, such ships need a high cubic capacity. Logs tend to damage the carrying ships, so these vessels are normally basic and cheap. *See Figs. 73, **138**.*

Fig. 73 Logs for export being handled at the port of Tauranga, New Zealand

Log grab Attachment to a crane, log stacker or fork-lift truck with two 'arms' which, when brought together, encompass almost completely a bundle of logs, enabling it to be lifted. The arms may be curved or straight. Also known as a **log gripper**.

Log grapple Attachment to a crane that consists of a pair of large pincers at the end of a wire. These grip the topmost logs of a strapped bundle of logs for the purpose of lifting.

Log handling When exported, logs are generally transported by lorry from the forest to the railhead where they are transferred to rail wagons. Where there is a river close to the place where the trees are felled, they may be floated downriver or loaded into barges and towed to a port for ocean transport by ship. Lorries may be known as log carriers or logging trucks. They have open beds with stanchions or uprights on each side to hold the logs in place, and may have an onboard grapple to enable the logs to be loaded or unloaded without any other equipment. Forest products terminals are areas of a port dedicated to forest products, including logs. These have equipment capable of lifting logs. *See* **Forest products terminal, Grapple, Log grab, Log stacker, Timber dogs** *and* **Tongs**. Logs are carried by sea in log carriers (*see* **Log carrier**).

Log stacker Vehicle dedicated to lifting and stacking logs. It is equipped with a log gripper that consists of two 'arms' which, when brought together, encompass a bundle of logs enabling it to be lifted. Log stackers are manufactured with various capacities. *See Figs. 73, 74.*

Fig. 74 Log stacker

Lo-lo Abbreviated form of lift-on/lift-off. *For definition, see* **Lift-on/lift-off**.

Longitude Distance East or West of the Greenwich meridian, measured in degrees, minutes and seconds.

Longitudinal bulkhead Vertical separation in a ship, which runs either along her entire length, such as the two bulkheads which separate side tanks from centre tanks in a tanker, or along part of the length, as with a centreline

Loose

bulkhead in a dry cargo ship, which does not continue under the hatchways; this type of bulkhead is constructed to provide additional longitudinal strength.

Loose Said of a consignment which consists of single pieces not bundled together. *See Fig. 75.*

Fig. 75 Steel universal columns, shipped loose

Low loader Road trailer with a flat bed used for the movement of exceptionally large and heavy pieces of cargo. Also known as a **lowboy**.

Lower hold Area of a ship's hold underneath the tween deck.

Lower tween deck Space for carrying cargo in a ship that has a lower hold and an upper hold. It is situated immediately above the lower hold and below the deck which divides the upper hold in two.

LPG Liquefied petroleum gas or liquid petroleum gas. *See* **Liquefied petroleum gas carrier (LPG carrier).**

LPG/ammonia carrier Dual-purpose tanker which is fully refrigerated and designed to carry ammonia in liquid form or liquefied petroleum gas. Cargo is carried in refrigerated tanks which are kept separate from the ship's hull by an insulating barrier so as to help maintain the low temperature.

Mafi flat

Luffing Vertical movement of the jib of a crane. In some cases, the whole of the jib is luffed, while in others a small part of the jib at the top is moved vertically. A luffing crane is a crane whose jib can be moved at different angles to the horizontal.

Lumber load line One of the lines painted on the sides of a ship, which shows the maximum depths to which that ship's hull may be immersed when arriving at, sailing through, or putting to sea in the different load line zones with a deck cargo of timber. The positioning of these lines is determined by the rules agreed at the International Conference on Load Lines, which have been ratified by many maritime countries. Also known as the timber load line.

MacGregor hatch Proprietary hatch cover widely used on dry cargo ships. These are a means of closing hatchways and made of steel sections which are designed and operated in different ways depending on the type of ship. *For various examples, see* **Folding hatch cover, Lift-away hatch cover, Piggy-back hatch cover, Rolling hatch cover, Sliding hatch cover** *and* **Stacking hatch cover**.

Mafi flat or **Mafi trailer** or **Mafi** Proprietary name for a type of roll trailer. *For definition, see* **Roll trailer**. It is towed by a **mafi tractor**. *See Figs. 76, 108.*

Fig. 76 Roll trailer, this one carrying aluminium billets

Magnet

Magnet   Device attached to a crane which is used for lifting scrap iron.

Malaccamax (ship)   Large deep-draughted ship being planned, so called because it is the largest size vessel capable of transiting the Malacca straits. There are two types of Malaccamax being considered, a **Malaccamax containership** with a capacity of about 18,000 TEUs, and a tanker, the **Malaccamax VLCC**.

Malt terminal   Terminal in a port dedicated to the handling and storage of malt, a product of barley used in brewing beer. This type of terminal is similar to the one handling grain but has specialised silo equipment because of the sensitivity to crushing. Distribution is effected by chute for lorries, barges or outward-bound ships. There may also be a bagging plant. Malt is also carried in general purpose containers fitted with liner bags.

Manifest   Document containing a full list of a ship's cargo, extracted from the bills of lading. A copy, known as the outward manifest, is lodged with the Customs authorities at the port of loading. A further copy, known as the inward manifest, is similarly lodged at the discharge port, with one copy going to the ship's agent so that the unloading of the ship may be planned in advance.

Marks and numbers   Markings distinctly displayed on goods being shipped, or on their packaging, for ease of identification. These include the port or place of destination and a package number, if there is more than one. In some cases, such as paper reels, the identity of the cargo is contained in a bar code label. See Fig. 77.

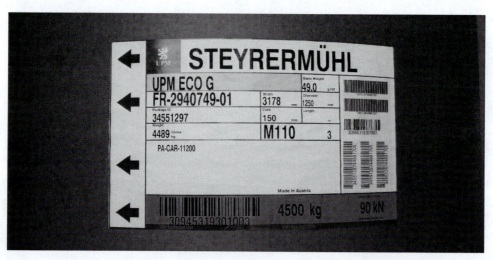

Fig. 77 Label on a paper reel identifying it within a shipment of reels

Maximum securing load (MSL) Maximum rated capacity of a device used to secure cargo.

Mechanical ventilation System of ventilating the holds of a ship whereby ventilators on deck are closed off, and air is circulated mechanically through the holds, being dried, if necessary, by dehumidifying equipment. This method of ventilating is useful when the outside air contains a high level of humidity, which would cause condensation damage to the cargo if introduced into the holds. This system is also known as forced ventilation.

Metacentre Point where a vertical line passing through a ship's centre of buoyancy when she is upright meets a vertical line passing through her new centre of buoyancy when she is heeling.

Metacentric height Distance between a ship's centre of gravity and her metacentre. The distance is critical since, if it is too small, the ship becomes unstable, having a tendency to roll slowly. Such a ship is said to be tender. If the metacentric height is too large, the ship tends to roll quickly. In this case, she is said to be stiff. The metacentric height is known as the GM where G is the centre of gravity and M is the metacentre.

Methane carrier Vessel designed to carry methane (liquefied natural gas). The gas is held in a liquid state by pressure and refrigeration. The cargo-carrying capability consists of special tanks whose upper sections often protrude above deck height in domed or cylindrical form. Also known as a liquefied natural gas (LNG) carrier or liquid natural gas carrier.

Mini-bulker Vessel of about 3,000 tonnes deadweight, which has the constructional features of a bulk carrier, having a single deck, hoppered holds and upper wing tanks, but which is smaller. As with the larger bulk carriers, the mini-bulker may be geared or gearless. Equally, it may have hatch covers capable of taking timber deck cargo or shipping containers.

Mobile crane General purpose crane capable of being moved from place to place. An example is a mobile crane used in a port, which is sometimes called a mobile harbour crane (MHC). Mobile cranes may be on wheels or mounted on crawlers and used for lifting, grabbing or drag line work. Some types are capable of lifting unusually heavy loads; such cranes are often hired by the day to load or discharge a small number of lifts too heavy for shore cranes or ship's gear. *See Figs. 36, 78.*

Mobile unloader

Fig. 78 Mobile crane; this model, in the Port of Antwerp, Belgium, is capable of handling cargo from ships up to Panamax size. It has a lifting capacity of 104 tonnes and a maximum radius of 48 metres. It is used for containers, dry bulk, general cargo and heavy lifts

Mobile unloader Type of ship unloader which is wheeled or on tracks and capable of being moved around a port wherever needed. It is typically used in ports where there is no dedicated terminal with its own fixed equipment. It allows flexibility but is slower. Mobile unloaders may be of the continuous or discontinuous type. Also called portable unloader. Performance is measured in tonnes per hour (TPH). See **Unloader** *and* **Continuous (ship) unloader (CSU)**.

Mobile harbour crane spreader Type of spreader used together with a mobile crane to lift containers. It is designed with weight-saving features to maximise its lifting capacity when used with a variety of cranes. *See Fig. 79*.

Mooring post

Fig. 79 Mobile harbour crane spreader

Mobile offshore drilling unit Self-propelled vessel used to drill offshore for oil.

Mobile unloader Type of ship unloader which is wheeled or on tracks and capable of being moved around a port wherever needed. It is typically used in ports where there is no dedicated terminal with its own fixed equipment. It allows flexibility but is slower. Mobile unloaders may be of the continuous or discontinuous type. Also called a portable unloader. Performance is measured in tonnes per hour (TPH). *See* **Unloader** *and* **Continuous (ship) unloader (CSU)**.

Mole Masonry structure projecting outwards from the shore, designed to protect the entrance to a port.

Mooring post Post, fixed to a quay, for securing mooring ropes. *See Fig. 80.*

Moulded breadth

Fig. 80 Self-tensioning mooring system

Moulded breadth   Maximum breadth of a ship, measured from the insides of her plating.

Moulded depth   Vertical distance from the keel to the uppermost deck, taken inside the ship's plating. Also, when a particular deck is specified, the moulded depth is the vertical distance to that deck. Also referred to as the depth moulded.

Multi-purpose cargo ship   Ship capable of handling several types of cargo, either in combination with each other or as full cargoes. There are several different multi-purpose ships, such as ore/bulk/oil carriers or barge/container ships.

Multi-purpose crane   Dockside crane capable of handling a wide variety of cargoes, such as general cargo, bagged or palletised goods, heavy lifts, bulk cargoes or containers. It is able to do so by varying the lifting attachments according to the product. Such attachments include grab, hook and spreader.

Multi-purpose supply vessel   Vessel used in a variety of ways to service and support the offshore oil industry. It is normally geared and may have a helicopter deck. It may be capable of firefighting and deep-water handling. Also known as a **multi-purpose service vessel**.

Multi-purpose terminal   Terminal in a port capable of handling and storing a wide variety of products whether in cases, on pallets, in bags or loose and unprotected. Such terminals are normally equipped with cranes which may have the capacity to lift unusually heavy loads. There is normally covered storage for cargoes that cannot be left out in the open. Some multipurpose terminals have ro-ro facilities.

Multideck ship   Ship with several decks or levels, most suited to carrying general cargo. This is because general cargo comprises many commodities, some heavier than others, all packed in various ways and often destined for a number of discharge ports; having several decks enables goods to be stowed in such a way that they do not damage each other, particularly by compression, and so that they are more easily accessible for discharging.

Narrow steel strip   *See* **Steel strip**. *See Fig. 81*.

Fig. 81 Narrow steel strip

Net

Net Device used for holding cargo while it is being lifted on and off a ship. It consists of a mesh made of rope or wire surrounded by a thicker rope or wire used for lifting cargo. It has an eye at each corner for lifting with a hook. Only cargo which is not easily susceptible to damage can be lifted in this way. Also known as a cargo net.

Net tonnage (NT) Figure representing the total of all the enclosed spaces within a ship available for cargo, arrived at by means of a formula which has as its basis the volume measured in cubic metres.

Newsprint Paper used for newspapers. It is transported in the form of paper reels and typically handled in ports and terminals using fork-lift trucks equipped with paper clamps.

Newsprint carrier Ship specially constructed to carry newsprint and associated products.

Nylon sling Sling used to put round cargo to avoid the sort of damage caused by a chain sling. A recent variation is sling tubing filled with thousands of strands of fibre to give it increased strength. *See Fig. 82.*

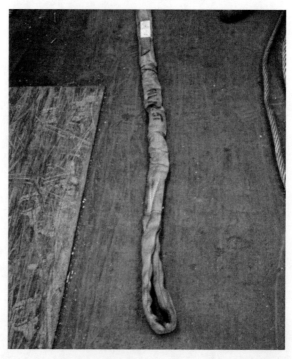

Fig. 82 Nylon round sling, used for sensitive cargoes; it has thousands of strands of fibre inside for strength

OBO *See* **Ore/bulk/oil carrier (OBO)**.

Oil barge   River barge designed for the carriage of oil cargoes.

Oil port   Port whose main or only type of cargo handled is oil, often with deep-water jetties to accommodate large oil tankers and with storage tanks and refineries.

Oil tanker   Ship designed for the carriage of oil in bulk, her cargo capacity consisting of several, or indeed many, tanks. Size and capacity of oil tankers range from the ultra-large crude carrier (ULCC) of over half a million tonnes deadweight to the small coastal tanker of a few hundred tonnes deadweight. Tankers load their cargo by gravity from the shore or by shore pumps and discharge using their own pumps.

Oil terminal   Terminal at a port whose main or only type of cargo handled is oil. It often has deep-water berths to accommodate large oil tankers and may have large storage tanks and refineries.

One-way pallet   Type of pallet in which the apertures intended to take the forks of a fork-lift truck are situated on one edge only. *See also* **Pallet, Two-way pallet** *and* **Four-way pallet**.

OO *See* **Ore/oil carrier (OO)**.

Open hatch bulk carrier   Type of bulk carrier whose hatch openings correspond in size to the floor of the holds. This allows the crane to position cargo for stowage directly into its location for the voyage and enables it to be lifted out without first being moved sideways. This configuration speeds up cargo handling and reduces damage. Such vessels are widely used for the carriage of reels of paper.

Open roadstead   Expanse of water situated off a port where ships are able to anchor safely but which is not sheltered.

Open-sided container or **open-side container**   Shipping container whose side is open to give unrestricted access for loading and discharging. The side of the container has removable steel grilles or gates and may have drop-down doors covering the lower part. The side is covered by a tarpaulin or tilt in transit. This type of container has two uses: for ventilation when carrying certain perishable goods and for loading and discharging at premises where side access is preferred. Also known as a produce carrier.

Open-top container

Open-top container Type of shipping container that has an open top covered by a tarpaulin instead of the solid roof found on general purpose containers. This is to enable cargoes to be carried in containers, and hence on containerships, which cannot be easily loaded through end doors and need to be loaded from the top. Timber and scrap metal are sometimes shipped in this way. Cargoes that are too high for general purpose containers can also be shipped in open-top containers, or **open-tops** as they are often called. These containers normally have end doors to give flexibility to loading and discharging operations. *See Figs. 83a, 83b.*

Fig. 83a A 40-foot open-top container

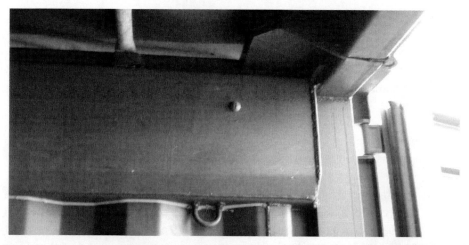

Fig. 83b This open-top container features a new development: just below the soft top is one of many fixings used to support a frame which converts the top into a solid one. This provides the operator with flexibility to use the box in whichever way dictated by the nature of the cargo

Open/closed shelter-deck ship or **open/closed shelter-decker** Shelter-deck ship which may be operated with the tonnage opening kept open or sealed up, depending on the trade in which she is employed. This type of ship was designed to have greater flexibility of use as either an open shelter-decker or a fully enclosed tween decker. *See also* **Shelter-deck ship**.

Optional cargo Cargo which is destined for one of the ship's discharge ports, the exact one not being known when the goods are loaded. It must therefore be stowed in such a position that it can be removed at any of a number of selected ports, known as **optional ports**, without disturbing other cargo.

Orange juice Product shipped in various forms: frozen concentrated orange juice has been heated to a high temperature to dehydrate it, reducing its volume by about seven times and thus making it cheaper to transport. Both frozen and chilled orange juice from concentrate are reconstituted with water at destination before being packaged for sale. Both these types, as well as orange juice not from concentrate, are chilled before being transported, or frozen into blocks, then defrosted before being packaged for sale. Orange juice is shipped in different ways, most often in bulk, in tankers, in tank containers or in large special containers in conventional ships.

Orange peel grab or **orange peel grapple** Type of grab with more than two parts, slung under a conventional crane. The parts are brought together to lift a bulk cargo. *See* **Grab**.

Ore carrier Large ship, generally gearless and with large hatchways, designed to be used for the carriage of various types of ore. Because of the high density of ore, ore carriers have a relatively high centre of gravity to prevent them being stiff when at sea, that is, rolling heavily with possible stress to the hull. This high centre of gravity is achieved by having relatively small cargo holds (small because the cargo takes up relatively little space) built over deep double-bottoms.

Ore/bulk/oil carrier (OBO) Large multi-purpose ship designed to carry cargoes of either ore or other bulk commodities or oil so as to reduce the time the ship would be in ballast if restricted to one type of commodity. The cargo is loaded into central holds and, if oil, into side tanks as well. This type of ship is sometimes referred to as a bulk/oil carrier.

Ore/oil carrier (OO) Ship designed to carry either ore or oil in bulk, the purpose being to reduce the time the ship would spend in ballast if restricted to

Ore pellet carrier

one commodity. Ore is carried only in the central holds, whereas oil is carried in wing tanks and in the central holds as well if required.

Ore pellet carrier Bulk carrier used principally for the carriage of iron ore which has been processed into pellets. This type of cargo is prone to spontaneous combustion and so the ship must be equipped with suitable fire-fighting equipment.

Out of gauge (OOG) Said of cargo which will not fit inside a container or whose dimensions exceed any of the external dimensions of the container on which it is carried. Also called dimensional, over-dimensional, oversized or over sized. *See Fig. 84.*

Fig. 84 Launches being loaded onto a ship; the one in the foreground is on a flatrack being moved on a roll trailer; note how the height of the launch exceeds the height of the flatrack ends

Outreach Maximum distance to which loading or discharging equipment can extend outwards to lift cargo. There are various points from which this distance may be measured, for example, from the quay wall or fendering, or the landside end of the jib of a shore crane, when it is also known as the crane's radius. The outreach can also describe the distance between the ship and shore, which a ramp can bridge. Also known as the reach or the radius. *See Fig. 85.*

Fig. 85 Outreach; the plate on this crane states the maximum lift at 42.5 metres is 12 tonnes and at 23.5 metres is 27 tonnes

Overall length   Maximum length between the extreme ends, forward and aft, of a ship. This measurement is often required to determine, for example, whether a ship can negotiate a particular lock or whether she can be accommodated at a specific berth. Also referred to as the length overall.

Over-clamp (to)   To squeeze a paper reel too hard with a clamp truck, thus ovalising it and causing problems for its eventual use.

Over-dimensional   *See* **Out of gauge (OOG)**.

Overheight cargo   Cargo in an open-top shipping container, which is higher than the top rails of the container. Such cargo is often difficult to accommodate in a containership as it cannot be overstowed. *See* **Overstow (to)**.

Overlength cargo   Cargo which is longer than a standard container. Such cargo is often difficult to accommodate in a containership.

Overside discharge   Removal of goods from a ship directly onto barges using the ship's cranes or derricks. When instructed to deliver cargo in this way, shipping lines often insert a clause in the bill of lading to the effect that

Over-sized

this will be carried out provided that sufficient barges are available. This is to ensure that there is no delay in the discharging of the ship.

Over-sized *See* **Out of gauge (OOG)**.

Overstow (to) To stow one item of cargo on top of another in a ship. It is important for a cargo superintendent to know whether a particular product may be overstowed by another, or at all, taking into consideration the safety of the cargo and of the ship when at sea.

Overwidth cargo Cargo in an open-top shipping container which is wider than the container. Such a cargo is often difficult to accommodate in a containership.

Packaged timber Method of presentation of timber for shipment, whereby it is strapped into large, uniform blocks capable of being handled and lifted quickly and economically into and out of modern timber carriers. This replaces the traditional practice of handling timber one piece at a time. *See Figs. 86a, 86b, 86c, 86d*.

Figs. 86a, 86b, 86c and 86d Packaged timber. The illustrations show packaged timber being discharged from a ship, then carried by fork-lift truck to an area of the quay to await onward transport by lorry

Packaged timber

Figs. 86b, 86c and 86d Packaged timber

Pallet

Pallet Flat tray on which goods, particularly those in boxes, cartons or bags, can be stacked. Its purpose is to facilitate the movement of such goods, mainly by the use of fork-lift trucks or hand pallet trucks whose forks are inserted under the top boards. Pallets may be constructed of different materials, mainly wood but sometimes plastic or metal. There are also variations in the design of the pallet (*see* **One-way pallet, Two-way pallet** *and* **Four-way pallet**). There are two principal sizes: the ISO pallet, which measures 1 by 1.2 metres, and the europallet, which measures 0.8 by 1.2 metres. There are some variations in the design of the pallet. *See Figs. 57, 89a, 89b, 91,* ***106, 119***.

Pallet cage Metal framework with a platform, which is attached to a crane, whose purpose is to enable a number of pallets to be loaded or discharged in one lift. A variation is a larger version, part of the side door of a pallet carrier. *See Figs.* ***87, 106***.

Fig. 87 Pallet/reefer with side door equipped with a spreader and pallet cage, providing protection against the weather while loading or unloading

Pallet carrier Ship designed to carry shipping containers and palletised goods. Although the ship is capable of carrying general cargo, the interior of the ship generally carries paper products on pallets. These are loaded through a side door, taken by pallet lift to the appropriate level and thence by fork-lift truck to the desired positions. The containers are carried on deck. Generally,

Pallet truck

such ships are refrigerated as they carry cargoes, such as fruit, which require refrigeration. They are then known as **pallet/reefers**. *See Fig. 87.*

Pallet elevator   Lifting device at the side of a pallet ship for taking pallets from the quay to the level in the ship where they will be stowed and vice versa. Palletised goods are brought alongside by a fork-lift truck and placed onto the elevator. This is raised or lowered to the appropriate level where small pallet trucks take the pallets and stow them. Also known as a **pallet lift**.

Pallet loading platform   Large slab, designed to be lifted by fork-lift truck, onto which a number of pallets are placed so as to move many pallets around in one lift. *See Fig. 88.*

Fig. 88 Pallet loading platforms; these have a safe working load of 25 tonnes

Pallet ship   Ship specially constructed with side ports and side hatches equipped with pallet elevators (also known as pallet lifts). Such ships specialise in carrying palletised goods and paper reels. *For the method of cargo handling, see* **Pallet elevator.**

Pallet truck   Small truck used to load pallets into shipping containers and to unload them. It is either manually operated or powered by electric motor. Like a fork-lift truck, it is equipped with forks that are inserted into or under the

Palletwide container

pallet. Typical capacities are between 1 and 2 tonnes. Also known as a **pallet transporter.** *See Figs. 89a, 89b.*

Fig. 89a Pallet truck

Fig. 89b Pallet truck

Palletwide container Container, at 2.5 metres, wider than the standard shipping container which measures 2.44 metres wide. It is designed to carry an optimum number of pallets, principally the europallet, which is 1.2 metres wide. A standard palletwide container will not fit into the cells of containerships and so is unsuitable for trades where shipping is restricted to cellular ships. A modification to the design to get round this problem resulted in the cellular palletwide container. Also known as a Euro container.

Panamax (ship) Ship capable of transiting the Panama Canal, as distinct from the Post-Panamax ships which are too large. There are two main categories:

Paper clamp

the Panamax bulk carrier of about 60,000–70,000 tonnes deadweight, and the Panamax containership of about 4,000–4,500 TEUs with 13 TEUs across the breadth. The maximum dimensions allowed for transiting the Panama Canal are 294.13 metres (965 feet) length, 32.31 metres (106 feet) breadth and 12.04 metres (39 feet 6 inches) draft in tropical fresh water.

Paper Commodity which may be transported unfinished in the form of bales of pulp (*see* **Paper pulp**), or finished in reels (*see* **Paper reel** *and* **Paper reel handling**).

Paper clamp Attachment to a fork-lift truck dedicated to the handling of paper reels. The two arms move inwards to grasp the roll before lifting. The most recent models are able to control the pressure exerted on the reel electronically according to the quality of the paper and the weight of the reel. This is to avoid damaging the reel by squeezing it too hard. *See Figs.* ***90a, 90b, 90c.***

Fig. 90a Paper clamp fitted to a clamp truck

Fig. 90b Paper clamp fork-lift attachment

Paper pulp

Fig. 90c Older form of paper clamp still in use

Paper pulp Raw material in the paper manufacturing process which is made by dissolving wood or recovered paper in water and chemicals. It is transported in bales, normally weighing 250kg each.

Paper reel Large roll of paper, normally wrapped in waterproof paper, with a wide variety of uses, including printing, such as newspapers and books, wallpaper, building materials, such as plasterboard, tissues and paper plates. Reels weigh from under 1 tonne to the most recent types which can weigh 4.5 tonnes. Also termed **paper roll**. *See* **Paper reel handling**. *See Figs. 34a, 34b, 41, 77, 90a, 90c, 91, 104.*

Fig. 91 Paper reels on a roll trailer

Paper reel handling Paper reels are normally handled at the port terminal at load and discharge ports by clamp trucks. These are fork-lift trucks fitted with clamps which are shaped to embrace the reels. These clamps are often intelligent, in that they are programmed not to squeeze the reels, or, as it is termed, over-clamp them. The reels are carried between the covered terminal and the ship by roll trailers which may be towed onto the ship and carried to the port of discharge. They may also be loaded onto cassettes and towed onto the ship using cassette trailers. Paper reels are carried in a variety of different ship types, mainly cassette carriers paper/container carriers, forest products carriers, newsprint carriers, open hatch bulk carriers and pallet ships. *See* **Paper/container carrier, Roll trailer, Intelligent clamp, Cassette, Cassette carrier, Clamp, Clamp truck, Core probe, Forest products carrier, Forest products terminal, Newsprint, Newsprint carrier, Open hatch bulk carrier, Over-clamp (to), Pallet ship, Paper clamp** *and* **Reel guard.**

Paper/container carrier Ship designed to carry shipping containers and paper, the latter normally in the form of reels. It has box-shaped holds suitable for the stowage of containers, a dehumidifying system to remove moisture from the holds, as dry conditions are necessary when carrying paper. The reels are loaded through doors in the side of the ship.

Paragraph ship Cargo-carrying ship so called because the regulations of various countries concerning the construction, equipment and manning of ships contain separate sections, or paragraphs, for ships of different gross tonnages. A paragraph ship is a ship whose gross tonnage is just below a certain figure which, if it were exceeded, would entail more stringent requirements and a higher running cost.

Parcel tanker Type of chemical tanker capable of carrying a number and variety of bulk liquids at the same time. This involves having a large number of segregated cargo tanks, often coated or constructed of stainless steel to ensure that the quality of the cargo is maintained, as well as a complex system of pipes to avoid contamination. Cargoes likely to be carried include coconut oil and palm oil, inorganic acids and cooled semi-gases.

Passenger/train/vehicle carrier Vessel having, typically, three decks onto which vehicles, both cars and trucks, are carried and having rails on several tracks allowing rail wagons to be transported. The vessel has overnight accommodation for passengers and may well have entertainment and

Passenger/vehicle ferry

shopping facilities on board. The vehicle decks are interconnected by internal ramps.

Passenger/vehicle ferry Vessel designed to carry passengers (with or without cars) and commercial vehicles with their drivers, usually on short sea crossings. Vehicles are driven on and off the ship on ramps and spend the voyage on special decks, with private cars normally kept separate from commercial vehicles.

Payload Maximum amount that a piece of equipment, for example, a crane, fork-lift or container, can handle. It is normally a weight expressed in tonnes. May be used as an equivalent to the safe working load.

Peak tank Small tank situated at the extreme forward end (fore peak tank) or after end (aft peak tank or after peak tank) of a ship. It normally holds water ballast and is used in this way to assist in the trim of the ship, that is, the relationship between the draught forward and the draught aft.

Pedestal crane or **pedestal mounted crane** Crane with a mounting consisting of a fixed pedestal or cylindrical column. Found on oil and natural gas platforms, this mounting is also used for deck cranes on ships: the pedestal can support one and sometimes two (twin) cranes.

Perishable goods Goods, notably foodstuffs, that are liable to decay if the conditions within the ship or shipping container in which they are being carried are not strictly controlled or, in some cases, if the voyage time is unduly extended. Perishable goods require refrigeration, ventilation or, in some cases, the use of a controlled atmosphere container.

Permanent dunnage *See* **Cargo battens**.

Phosphate *See* **Fertiliser**.

Phosphoric acid carrier Tanker designed to carry phosphoric acid, a substance used for fertilisers. Cargo tanks are required to be of high grade stainless steel which has a resistance to pitting. The heating coils needed for this cargo need to be corrosion-resistant. There is a need to keep this cargo circulating as a sediment is otherwise created.

Photo gate Structure at a container terminal equipped with cameras used to record the details and condition of containers when arriving and departing by road. *See Fig. 92. Also called* **photo portal**.

Pilotage

Fig. 92 Photo gate or photo portal

Piggy-back The carriage of road trailers on special rail wagons. The tractor may remain with the trailer or may be detached and not carried, according to the particular system. The trailer is unaccompanied. Rail wagons may be flat or may have a well into which the trailer is lowered so as to come within a country's loading gauge. This method of transport is used for medium to long distance when it is desirable for economic and/or environmental reasons.

Piggy-back hatch cover Arrangement of weather deck hatch covers whereby one panel of a two-panel hatch cover is stowed on top of the other when opened. Hydraulically operated, one panel is raised vertically and the second panel slides underneath it; both panels are then rolled to the side or the end of the hatchway, depending on the design of the ship. This type of hatch cover is found on bulk carriers and multi-purpose ships.

Pilotage The act, carried out by a pilot, of assisting the master of a ship in navigation when entering or leaving a port or in confined waters. The pilot is a qualified person, usually an experienced mariner familiar with the particular

Pipe hook

port or place. The term pilotage is also sometimes used to mean **pilotage dues** or **pilotage charges**. These are paid for by the shipowner for the services of a pilot and normally charged on the basis of a lump sum depending on the gross tonnage of the ship or an amount per 100 gross tonnes.

Pipe hook   Attachment to a crane for lifting pipes. It may be teflon-coated to avoid damage when coming into contact with the pipe's surface. *See Figs. 62, 93*.

Fig. 93 Pipe hook; this one is teflon-coated, for use with coated pipes, so as not to damage the inside coating of the pipe

Plastics terminal   Terminal in a port dedicated to the handling and storage of plastics in bulk or in bags. The product may be in granular or powder form and storage is in silos for bulk cargoes or warehouses when bagged. Distribution facilities include bagging, palletisation and transfer from silo to bulk vehicles or bulk containers and vice versa.

Plate clamp   Device, several of which are placed along the edges of steel plates, used when lifting. As the load is lifted, the clamps grip the edges of the plates.

Plate hooks Attachments to a crane in the form of U-shaped hooks placed in pairs along the length of a steel plate and used to lift the plates. *See Figs.* ***94a, 94b***.

Fig. 94a Pair of plate hooks; this pair has a lifting capacity of 3 tonnes

Fig. 94b This spreader is being used to help lift long length steel plates; hanging from the spreader are chains linked to plate hooks

Platform

Platform Flat surface in a ship on which vehicles can be moved from one level to another, for example from the tween deck to the weather deck. Unlike ramps, platforms are raised and lowered horizontally. This is effected by hydraulics, either with wires or chains.

Platform flat Effectively a shipping container without sides, ends or a roof. Normally 20 or 40 feet long, they are used for awkwardly shaped cargoes which cannot fit on or in any other type of container. They are sometimes termed an artificial tween deck as this is what is achieved when several platform flats are placed end to end in a ship. *See Fig. 95.*

Fig. 95 A 40-foot platform flat

Platform supply vessel Vessel utilised to supply the offshore oil industry.

Plimsoll Line Summer load line of a ship, that is, the line painted on the sides of a ship, which shows the maximum depth to which the ship's hull may be immersed when in a summer zone. The line is marked with an S. Also referred to as summer marks.

Pneumatic crane Crane powered by a pneumatic motor, that is, a motor powered by pressurised air or gas. *See Fig. 36.*

Pneumatic unloader Type of continuous ship unloader. It consists of a pipe with a nozzle which is lowered into a free-flowing cargo in the hold of a ship and discharges it using suction. Typical products handled include grain and cement. Also known as a vacuum unloader. Performance is measured in tonnes per hour (TPH).

Pontoon   Flat-bottomed vessel with a shallow draught.

Pontoon crane   Type of mobile crane. It is fixed to a pontoon or shallow barge and is used for loading or unloading vessels in situations where there is no shore gear.

Pontoon hatch cover   Hatch cover consisting of a single slab that is lifted off when access to the hold is required. It may be lifted by shore cranes or the ship's gear and stacked with others out of the way until the hatch is to be closed. This type of hatch cover is typically found on cellular container-ships but is also fitted to multi-purpose and heavy lift ships. This hatch cover is also termed a lift-away hatch cover.

Pontoon hatch cover crane   Type of crane found on some vessels which is capable of lifting a pontoon hatch cover (also called a lift-away hatch cover). This may be a travelling crane that moves along the ship to reach the appropriate hatch.

Port or **port side**   The left side of a ship when viewed facing forwards.

Port mark   The name of the discharge port marked on goods or their packaging to help prevent them from being discharged at the wrong port or, if they are, to enable them to be re-routed to the correct destination.

Portable unloader   *See* **Mobile unloader**.

Portainer   Range of proprietary dockside container cranes, typically having an 'A' frame. There are various types, each of which is suitable for a different size of ship. The latest generation can handle Super-Post-Panamax vessels by means of greater outreach and height.

Portal   *See* **Radiation portal**.

Portal crane   Crane which is supported on a portal or set of legs. Portal cranes can be found on the quay, in which case they are designed to allow rail wagons and vehicles, particularly those carrying containers, to pass underneath for the purposes of being loaded or unloaded. They are also found on ships where they straddle the holds.

Porthole container or **porthole type container**   Type of insulated container that has two apertures, known as portholes, through which air of the correct temperature for the cargo is delivered from, and returned to, a terminal's refrigeration unit or from a clip-on unit.

Post-Panamax (ship)

Post-Panamax (ship) Ship so large that it cannot transit the Panama Canal. There are three main categories: **Post-Panamax bulk carrier**, **Post-Panamax tanker** and **Post-Panamax containership** of about 7,000–9,000 TEUs with 17 or more TEUs across the breadth. The largest of these is sometimes referred to as Super-Post-Panamax containerships or **Post-Panamax plus containerships**.

Post-Panamax crane Crane capable of being used to load or discharge a Post-Panamax containership. A Super-Post-Panamax crane is a crane big enough to load or discharge a Super-Post-Panamax containership.

Potash See **Fertiliser**. See Fig. 96.

Fig. 96 The Port of Portland's (Oregon, USA) Terminal 5. In the foreground, the Portland Bulk Terminal potash export facility. In the background is Columbia Grain's Terminal 5 grain export facility

Power pack Transportable self-contained refrigeration unit powered by its own generator. It is designed to provide power for refrigerated shipping containers where there is inadequate electrical power, whether in port or at sea. It is built into a 20-foot container, thus enabling it to be carried and handled in the same way.

Pre-sling (to) To place goods in slings that are left in position and used for the loading to, and discharge from, a ship. This is a form of unit load, the purpose of which is to simplify handling and increase the rate of loading and discharging.

Pulp clamps

Pre-slinging is used for products which cannot be palletised or containerised. It is a requirement of some importing countries for certain products.

Preventer Rope or wire attached at one end to a ship's derrick head and at the other end secured to the deck of the ship, in order to relieve the strain on the mast.

Produce carrier Shipping container whose side is open to give unrestricted access for loading and discharging. The side of the container has removable steel grilles or gates and may have drop-down doors covering the lower part. This type of container has two uses: for ventilation when carrying certain perishable goods and for loading and discharging at premises where side access is preferred. Also known as an open-sided container or open-side container.

Product carrier or **products carrier** Tanker designed to carry a variety of liquid products varying from crude oil to clean and dirty petroleum products, acids, other chemicals and even molasses. The tanks are coated, this being a requirement of some of the products carried, and the ship may have equipment designed for the loading and unloading of cargoes with a high viscosity.

Propane carrier Ship designed to carry propane in liquid form. The propane is carried in tanks within the holds; it remains in liquid form by means of pressure and refrigeration. Such ships are also suitable for the carriage of butane.

Pulp clamps Large metal plates, attachments to a fork-lift truck, which are used to lift bales of pulp by squeezing them together. *See Fig. 97*.

Fig. 97 Fork-lift pulp clamp capable of lifting 2 units of 2 tonnes each x 2 high

Pump truck *See* **Hand pallet truck**.

Purchase Gain in pull or power of a derrick obtained by using two blocks, an upper and lower one, with the rope or wire traversing each one a certain number of times. The gain is roughly equivalent to the number of parts of the rope going through the lower block. Thus, in the case of a gun tackle purchase, the rope is in two parts and the pull doubled; the rope in a double purchase configuration is in four parts, roughly quadrupling the pull. This makes lifting easier but the safe working load of the derrick should nevertheless not be exceeded.

Pure car carrier (PCC) Ship designed to carry unaccompanied new cars, normally in large numbers over long distances. Replacing the bulk carriers that were originally used to carry cars on the outward leg and bulk cargoes on the return leg, the pure car carrier has ro-ro type ramps, which give access to a number of decks, typically 12 or 13. Some car carriers have the flexibility to carry other vehicles such as trucks, trailers and buses, and these are sometimes referred to as vehicle carriers or **pure car and truck carriers (PCTC)**. *See Figs. 98, 120.*

Fig. 98 Pure car and truck carrier in the background

Pushed barge *See* **Barge**.

Pusher or **pusher tug** River tug which moves barges by pushing rather than towing. *See Fig. 99.*

Fig. 99 Pusher tug on the Mississippi River, USA

Quarter ramp Ramp fitted to a ro-ro ship, normally at the stern, which makes an angle of about 45 degrees with the axis (fore and aft) direction of the ship and which connects the ship to the shore. Its purpose is to allow the ship to moor alongside the quay and enable wheeled cargo to be driven on and off without special quay facilities. When not in use, the ramp is stowed upright, either straight or folded depending on its length and the number of sections which comprise it. Generally, quarter ramps are accompanied by separate watertight doors.

Quarter-deck Upper deck of a ship at the stern end. A raised quarter-deck ship is one whose quarter-deck has been raised to provide more cargo-carrying capacity.

Quartz sand terminal Terminal in a port dedicated to the handling and storage of quartz sand, used primarily in glass-making. Quartz sand is shipped in bulk, loaded by means of a conveyor and discharged by crane. Storage is in silos.

Quay Solid structure alongside a navigable waterway to which ships are moored for the purposes of loading and discharging.

Quick release gear Type of ship's hook which opens automatically to release the goods when they are landed. Examples are can hooks and plate clamps.

Quoin

Quoin Softwood wedge used to chock off casks or other rounded pieces of cargo.

Radiation detection equipment Equipment installed, for example, at ports or rail yards, to counter terrorist threats. There are various types of equipment: mobile, hand-held and fixed. The fixed type consists of a portal through which shipping containers are driven. Also known as **radiation monitoring equipment**. *See Fig. 100.*

Fig. 100 Radiation detection system; this one is mounted on a spreader

Radiation portal Structure consisting of two uprights which is capable of detecting nuclear or radiological material in a vehicle or shipping container whilst in motion. Such portals are typically found at borders and seaports. The system that detects nuclear and radiological materials and issues an alert is termed a **radiation portal monitor**.

Radio frequency identification (RFID) Means of tracking cargo or containers using an electronic tag, which bounces a signal off a satellite to determine the precise location of the object to which it is attached. Tags are deactivated on arrival of the cargo at the destination. When used with containers, the tag is attached to the door or to the inside of the container, depending on the exact type. This technology is used not only for tracking but also to help increase the effectiveness of the supply chain.

Radius (of a crane) *See* **Outreach**. *See Fig. 85.*

Rail clamp Attachment to a crane that sits across a number of rails and is clamped to the heads of the rails to enable them to be lifted. Several of these are used along the length of the rails. *See Fig.* **101**.

Fig. 101 Rail clamp; this one has a lifting capacity of 6 tonnes

Rail-mounted crane Crane which is mounted on rails allowing it to move typically along the quay. A **rail-mounted gantry crane** moves up and down rows of containers, for example in a container yard. *See Figs.* **29, 65, 102**.

Fig. 102 Container gantry crane; this model is rail-mounted

Raised quarter-deck ship

Raised quarter-deck ship Ship whose upper deck is raised at the stern end in order to increase cargo capacity.

Ramp Inclined plane fitted to a ro-ro ship over which vehicles are driven and which either connects the ship to the shore (exterior ramp) or connects one level or deck of the ship to another (interior ramp or internal ramp). Depending on the type of ship and the particular requirement, a ramp may be at the front (bow ramp), side (side ramp) or rear (stern ramp). It may be fixed in one direction or, particularly in the case of stern ramps, may be angled (quarter ramp) or capable of swinging from one direction to another to suit individual berthing positions (slewing ramp and semi-slewing ramp). The ramp is folded against the side of the ship when not in use and, in many designs of ship, acts as a watertight door when closed. Operationally, the important characteristics of a ramp are: its width – it must be capable of accommodating the widest type of cargo envisaged; the load carrying capacity, that is, the maximum weight imposed on the ramp at one time; differences in level, which occur with changes of draught during loading and unloading: this determines the length of ramp required.

Ramp/hatch cover Vehicle ramp in the deck of a ship, which also acts as a watertight hatch cover. This arrangement avoids the need for a separate hatch cover. A ramp/hatch combination is a configuration where a separate hatch cover pivots either upwards from one end or sideways to allow the ramp to be positioned. When the ramp is movable, the hatch cover and the ramp are positioned simultaneously. If the ramp is fixed, the hatch cover operates independently.

Ramping system Method of loading cars into standard shipping containers. This consists of a steel framework and ramps which may be fixed within the container, or removable. When removable, the apparatus is designed to fold up so that a large number can be returned in a container on the return leg. When two cars are to be shipped in a container, one is secured on the floor of the container while the other is driven up on ramps and secured, remaining at an angle above the first. Ramping systems also exist for loading three or four cars in a container.

Reach (of a crane) Maximum distance to which loading or discharging equipment can extend outwards to lift cargo. There are various points from which this distance can be measured, for example, from the quay wall or fendering, or the landside end of the jib of a shore crane. Also known as the outreach.

Reach stacker Type of frontlift truck with a telescopic boom and top-lift attachment used for lifting containers and stacking them. Its design enables it

Reach stacker

to reach beyond the first row to pick up a container. This is particularly useful in terminals where space does not permit vehicles to pass between every row of containers. Also known as a boom handler, and also spelled **reachstacker**. See Figs. **27a**, **103a**, **103b**.

Fig. 103a Reach stacker

Fig. 103b Reach stacker lifting a 25-tonne superpack of aluminium billets

Recyclable

Recyclable Said of a material which is capable of being recycled into usable products by means of one or more processes. *See* **Biomass** *and* **Glass** *for examples.*

Redwood Scale Scale which measures the viscosity of oils, for example, fuel oil and diesel oil. The unit of measurement is the second: the greater the number of seconds, the higher the viscosity of a grade of oil.

Reefer (ship) Refrigerated ship. *For definition, see* **Refrigerated ship**.

Reefer container, reefer box, reefer *See* **Refrigerated container.**

Reefer plug Plug in a ship to which an integral refrigerated container is connected in order to power the container's inbuilt generator, so as to maintain the correct temperature for the cargo.

Reel guard Curved sheet, typically made of fibre glass, placed around a paper reel to protect it from contact damage, particularly from fork-lift trucks. *See Fig. 104.*

Fig. 104 Larger size paper reels weighing 4.5 tonnes each, with reel guards

Refrigerated cargo pallet carrier Vessel used for the carriage of refrigerated cargoes in insulated hold spaces, which can also be used to carry palletised goods.

Refrigerated ship

Refrigerated container Insulated shipping container used for the carriage of goods requiring refrigeration in transit, such as fruit, vegetables, dairy products and meat. It is fitted with a refrigeration unit that is connected to the carrying ship's electrical supply. While the container is on the road, it can be fitted with a demountable generator. The refrigerated container is also known as a reefer container, reefer box or simply reefer. A variation of the refrigerated container is the high cube reefer, which has a higher cubic capacity than the standard size reefer container and thus can carry a greater volume of cargo. The extra capacity is achieved either by increasing the height of the container or by designing it so that the space taken by the clip-on diesel generator is over and above the standard dimensions of the container. *See Fig. 105.*

Fig. 105 Rear view of a refrigerated container (reefer) showing the refrigeration unit; this model is a 45-foot high cube reefer

Refrigerated ship Ship equipped with a refrigerating system for carrying perishable goods such as fruit, vegetables, meat and fish. Basic constructional features are similar to those of a general cargo ship. Refrigeration of cargo spaces is effected by circulating cool air at temperatures appropriate to the particular cargo. The cargo spaces are insulated, normally with aluminium or galvanised steel, to assist in maintaining the desired temperature. When dedicated to the fruit trade, this type of ship is sometimes called a fruit carrier. *See Fig. 106.*

Refrigerated trailer vessel

Fig. 106 Kiwi fruit in cartons on pallets being loaded on a refrigerated ship in Tauranga, New Zealand; the pallets are placed in pallet cages, a number of which can be seen under the hooks of the cranes

Refrigerated trailer vessel Vessel with decks on which refrigerated trailers are carried. Essentially it is a ro-ro ship with a large number of electrical socket connections to enable the trailer's refrigeration units to be operated. When carrying shiploads of meat, these ships are referred to as **refrigerated meat carriers**.

Removable deck Deck of a ship which is capable of being removed and stowed out of the way. This type of deck is found in some early car carriers and is removed when the ship is carrying a bulk cargo. More recent car carriers tend to have decks which fold away when not in use, rather than those which have to be completely removed.

Reserve buoyancy Volume of watertight space of a ship above the waterline, providing safety for the ship while at sea.

Rigger Person who rigs any type of lifting equipment, such as a crane or a ship's derrick, in readiness for hoisting cargo.

Rigging Arranging of the guys, that is, the wires or ropes which are attached to a ship's derrick and which are used to control it.

Roll trailer

Rigging screw Screw which applies tension to ropes or chains used for lashing cargo.

Rise of floor Distance from a horizontal line extending outwards to the ship's side from the centre line of a ship to the lowest point of the ship's side. This distance or height equates to a sloping of the hull intended to allow drainage of liquids.

Roads or **roadstead** Expanse of water situated off a port where ships are able to anchor safely.

Roll-on/roll-off System of loading and discharging a ship whereby the cargo is driven on and off on ramps. A ship designed to handle cargo in this way is known as a **roll-on/roll-off ship** or ro-ro ship. *See Figs.* **14**, **56**, **131**.

Roll-on/roll-off barge Barge which has a ramp used for driving cargo on and off. Also known as a ro-ro barge.

Roll trailer Trailer used to convey goods such as packaged timber or paper reels onto ro-ro ships. This type of trailer is towed onto the ship, secured on a vehicle deck and towed off at the port of destination, after which the goods are transferred to other modes of transport such as road trailers or rail wagons. Known widely as a Mafi, although this is a proprietary name. *See Figs.* **17**, **67a**, **84**, **91**, **107a**, **107b**.

Fig. 107a Roll trailer; this one is 62 feet long with a 90-tonne payload

Rolling cargo

Fig. 107b A 220-tonne (220 tonnes carrying capacity) roll trailer, 42 feet 6 inches long

Rolling cargo Cargo which is on wheels, such as trucks or trailers, and which can be driven or towed onto a ship. This term is normally used with reference to a ship that has ro-ro facilities, such as ramps and vehicle decks. Sometimes termed **rollable cargo.**

Rolling hatch cover Type of hatch cover typically found on the weather deck of bulk carriers. When opened to allow access to the hold, this type of cover is designed to be stowed either in a transverse direction, in which case it is known as a side-rolling hatch cover, or longitudinally, when it is called an end-rolling cover. Depending on the design of the ship, each hatch may have one or two covers.

Ro-pax vessel Ro-ro/vehicle/passenger ferry.

Rope sling Piece of rope whose ends are joined together so that it forms a loop. It is slung around cargoes in bags or bales, for example, so that these can be lifted. Also known simply as a sling.

Ro-ro tractor Vehicle which is used to pull various types of trailer in a ro-ro terminal, and on and off ro-ro ships. *See Fig. 108.*

Ro-ro/container vessel

Fig. 108 Ro-ro tractor. This model has a fifth-wheel capacity of 37 tonnes

Ro-ro/container vessel   Ship which carries shipping containers and has cell guides within which to accommodate them; it also has decks to take ro-ro cargo. Also known as a con-ro ship. *See Fig. **109**.*

Fig. 109 ACL ro-ro/container vessel 'Atlantic Cartier'; note the cell guides on deck

Ro-ro/vehicle/passenger ferry

Ro-ro/vehicle/passenger ferry or **ro-ro/passenger ferry** Vessel designed to carry passengers with or without cars, commercial vehicles with their drivers and unaccompanied ro-ro cargo on trailers. All vehicles are driven on and off the ship on ramps and spend the voyage on special decks, often segregated according to the type of vehicle. This type of ship is normally used on short sea routes. Also known as a ro-pax vessel.

Rubber-tyred gantry (RTG) crane Type of gantry crane which is not rail-mounted so that it is not confined to one area of a terminal and can be moved around as required. *See Fig. 110.*

Fig. 110 Rubber-tyred gantry cranes

Runner Rope or wire which goes through a pulley and which is used in order to vary the lifting power of a derrick.

Safe working load (SWL) The maximum load which can safely be borne by a lifting or handling device such as a crane or winch. It is generally marked clearly on the equipment and should not be exceeded.

Safety cage Metal framework which can be lifted on and off the deck of a ship to allow work to be carried out without the fear of falling overboard. *See Fig. 111.*

Salt handling

Fig. 111 Safety cage

Sag (to) Said of a ship, that the centre is depressed below the level of the two ends. This bending of the ship's plating is caused by the effect of waves on the ship when at sea or by the uneven distribution of weight along its length. It may result in damage or distortion to the hull.

Sail-assisted bulk carrier Bulk carrier that is conventionally constructed except for having two rectangular rigid sails mounted athwartships in a position forward of, and consequently out of the way of, the forward-most hatch covers. Savings in fuel and exhaust gas emission combined with greater stability are claimed for this design, which involves an on-board computer determining the most efficient angle for the sails.

Salt (common salt or NaCl) Mineral which is shipped in bulk in large quantities annually. It is used in food manufacture, in water softening and in many manufacturing processes. It is also spread on icy roads to melt the ice.

Salt handling Salt is loaded by conveyor to a spout and discharged by grab to hoppers positioned above trucks or rail wagons. It is shipped in bulk carriers. *See Fig. 112*.

145

Salt water arrival draught (SWAD)

Fig. 112 Salt

Salt water arrival draught (SWAD) Maximum draught in salt (sea) water. This figure may be required from a vessel advising her ETA at a port.

Samson-post Short, heavy mast, often one of a pair, situated between the hatches of a ship, which supports the derrick posts. They are usually associated with heavy-lift derricks and found on larger ships.

Sand and gravel terminal Normally an open area at the port, this type of dedicated terminal takes sea-dredged sand and aggregates from dredgers of various types. These products are washed and screened before being loaded to lorry or barge for distribution to the construction industry.

Sand bar Sandbank which forms at the mouth of a river and which very often limits the size of ships able to reach up-river destinations. In many cases, ships bound for an up-river discharge port have to lighten, that is, discharge some of their cargo to barges or small ships before being able to navigate over a sand bar and reach the port. Equally, ships loading at an up-river port may be able to load only part of the cargo, the balance being taken on board after the ship has cleared the bar.

Sand dredger or **sand carrier** Vessel designed to remove sand from the sea bed or from a river bed. This is often done at or near a port to increase the depth of water or to restore it to its previous depth. This enables access to a port by vessels with deeper draught or allows a ship to carry a greater weight of cargo. The methods of dredging are by suction, buckets and grab. The suction method uses a pipe and a submersible pump to suck sand. The bucket method uses a continuous supply of buckets that reach to the sea bed and scrape up the sand or aggregate. A grab may also be employed on the end of a crane. All three operations transfer the sand or aggregate into the hold or into hoppers and thence to barges for removal. In some cases, the ship's hold may have a bottom opening through which the sand is dropped out at sea.

SBM *See* **Single buoy mooring (SBM)**.

SBT *See* **Segregated ballast tank (SBT)**.

Scow Flat-bottomed lighter. Also called scow barge.

Scrap Metal intended for recycling. It comes from various products which can no longer be used, as diverse as old or damaged vehicles, white goods, constructional material, and drinks and other cans. It may be ferrous, that is, containing iron, or non-ferrous. Scrap is used to a greater or lesser extent in the production of new metals. Ferrous metal scrap is used in the production of steel. Traditional steel mills may use a proportion of scrap in their production. Some more recent mills, known as mini mills, use only scrap.

Scrap handling Scrap may be delivered to and from the port by road or rail. Lorries and rail wagons are of various types, depending on the size of the pieces being carried. These may be loose or crushed and compressed into bales. Ports may have terminals dedicated to the handling and storage of scrap metal. Generally, facilities are few, with an open space capable of allowing scrap of several different basic types to be piled awaiting distribution. Shore cranes are needed to discharge the ships using grabs or magnets. Loose scrap is normally shipped in bulk carriers. Bales may also be shipped in this way or in containers, especially for smaller quantities.

Screw conveyor Type of loading and discharging equipment consisting of a tubular section containing a 'screw' which revolves. It draws in the cargo and carries it to or from the ship, or to or from a waiting vehicle or rail wagon. Screw conveyors, similar to other conveyors, may be horizontal, vertical or along an incline. This type of continuous equipment is typically used for cement but can also handle other cargoes, such as coal. Performance is measured in tonnes per hour (TPH).

Seal (of a container)

Seal (of a container) Security device attached to the doors of a shipping container. Seals may be made of metal or plastic and are of two basic types: barrier and indicative. The barrier type is made of metal and can consist of a cable made into a loop, which can be self-locking, or a steel bolt. The indicative type seal is a plastic strip whose main purpose is to provide a visual indication as to whether tampering has taken place. If the seal is intact on arrival at the destination, this is virtual proof that the container has not been opened while in transit. *See also* **Barrier seal**, **Bolt seal**, **Cable seal**, **Indicative seal** *and* **Strip seal**. *See Fig. 113.*

Fig. 113 Container security; this container has two places where seals can be affixed: the normal place is the horizontal bar, the new position is in the locking rod (the vertical bar)

Seasonal tropical zone One of the several geographic areas, defined by the International Convention on Load Lines, where, during certain periods of the year which may vary according to the particular zone, a ship's hull may be immersed no deeper than its tropical load line.

Seasonal winter zone One of the several geographic areas, defined by the International Convention on Load Lines, where, during certain periods of the year which may vary according to the particular zone, a ship's hull may be immersed no deeper than its winter load line.

Self-propelled barge

Seconds Unit of measurement of the viscosity of oils such as fuel oil or diesel oil, used in the Redwood Scale. The higher the number of seconds, the greater the viscosity of the oil. Often abbreviated to **secs**.

Secure (to) To prevent a cargo from shifting in transit by lashing it to the ship or to the shipping container or vehicle by means of wires, chains, rope or straps.

Securing point Place on a piece of cargo, or on a part of the ship or container, where straps or chains or other means of securing are to be attached to keep the cargo from moving while in transit.

Segregated ballast tank (SBT) Tank in a tanker which is used for water ballast only. There is thus no risk of the cargo being mixed with ballast, with resulting pollution when the latter is pumped out.

Self-loading trailer *See* **Side-loading trailer**.

Self-loading vessel Vessel which has its own means of loading cargo. An example is a self-sustaining containership.

Self-propelled barge Manned barge which has its own motor and means of control. Such barges tend to operate singly for the purpose of carrying cargo in contrast to the so-called dumb barges, which have no engine and which are towed or pushed together with others in a string or train. Self-propelled barges have the disadvantage of having less usable cargo space than dumb barges. *See Fig. 114*.

Fig. 114 Self-propelled barge on the Mississippi, USA, carrying dredging pipes

Self-propelled trailer

Self-propelled trailer Trailer which has its own power, that is, it does not require a tractor or fork-lift truck. The motor is located under the bed of the trailer. It is used in confined yards and warehouses.

Self-sustaining ship Containership which has its own crane or cranes for loading and discharging shipping containers, enabling the ship to serve ports that do not have adequate, or indeed any, lifting equipment.

Self-trimming ship or **self-trimmer** Ship whose holds are shaped in such a way that a bulk cargo loaded into it will level itself.

Self-unloader Bulk carrier which is equipped with gear to enable it to discharge without using shore equipment. Vessels of this type are used in the iron ore and coal trades. Typical gear is a boom conveyor which is capable of a high rate of discharging from ship to shore or from ship to ship. Often this is fed by opening gates on the floor of the holds, thus allowing the cargo to drop onto conveyor belts. It is then taken to one end where it is elevated to deck level by mechanical or pneumatic means. Barges used in these trades are also self-unloaders. *See Figs. 24a,* **115**.

Fig. 115 Self-unloader

Semi-slewing ramp *See* **Slewing ramp** *for definition.*

Semi-trailer Road trailer which has rear wheels but no front wheels. It is pulled along by a tractor unit, which has a set of rear wheels that act as the trailer's front wheels. When not being towed, it has legs that fold down to support the front end.

Separation Means of identifying separate consignments, particularly when there are several of the same commodity, so that they are not mixed or discharged at the wrong port. This is achieved by, for example, painting different colour marks on the cargo or putting tarpaulins, timber or mats, known as **separation mats**, between consignments. *See Figs.* **116, 127**.

Shackle

Fig. 116 Separation mat

Shackle Piece of iron used to link together two lengths of chain or a length of chain to a block, a mast or to the deck. It is normally U-shaped and has a pin that slots through the two ends and which is either screwed in or secured with a device called a forelock. Variations include D-shaped shackles and those which are used to take several eyes, which are round-sided and known as bow shackles. *See Fig. 117.*

Fig. 117 Shackles of different sizes corresponding to lifting capacities ranging from 3 tonnes to 75 tonnes

Shears or **shear-legs** Lifting apparatus, having two uprights separated at the bottom but joined at the top, used for heavy weights. Sometimes spelled **sheers** or **sheer-legs**.

Sheave Pulley wheel used on a derrick.

Sheep carrier Ship used for the carriage of livestock, mainly sheep. Many are converted from oil tankers and dry cargo ships, although a few have been built for the purpose. Ships which have been converted have essentially only had livestock decks added; these consist of weather-protected pens in which the livestock are carried. Also known as a livestock carrier.

Shelter-deck ship or **shelter-decker** Ship which has a deck, called the shelter-deck, above its main deck. The original purpose was to enable the ship to benefit from a lower registered tonnage since the shelter-deck space would not be included provided there was a small opening, known as the tonnage opening, in the upper deck. More recently, such ships have been assigned alternative tonnages and have a tonnage mark painted on their sides. If this mark is submerged, the ship's higher registered tonnage is used for the purpose of determining port charges; if not submerged, the lower tonnage applies.

Shifting boards Boards that are fitted longitudinally, that is, in a fore and aft direction, along the holds of a ship when carrying free-flowing cargoes such as grain. They are designed to prevent the cargo shifting from side to side, particularly when the ship is rolling heavily, as she would become dangerously unstable. Some vessels have longitudinal bulkheads permanently fitted in their holds and these obviate the need for shifting boards.

Ship arrester Barrier in a lock which prevents a ship from colliding with lock gates if unable to stop in time. This barrier is raised when the ship is ready to exit the lock. *See Fig. 72b.*

Ship canal Artificial waterway constructed either to provide shipping with shorter distances between ports or to enable ocean-going ships to penetrate inland to industrial areas.

Ship routing Service offered by a government department or private company whereby a shipowner or ship operator is provided with a route for his or her ship, devised by means of up-to-date weather predictions, which avoids severe weather conditions such as storms, fog and ice. This route is normally not the most direct but is expected to take less time as it avoids conditions that would require a reduction in speed. Additionally, the risks of heavy weather damage and, in extreme cases, of injury to the crew, are reduced. A fee is charged for this service. Also known as weather routing.

Shiploader Shore equipment used to load bulk cargoes such as fertiliser or iron ore. It normally consists of a conveyor system linked to a chute or spout which directs the cargo into the holds of a ship. This method is normally associated with a high rate of loading. It may be either the travelling type on rails or mobile, in other words on wheels and so capable of going anywhere in the port. *See Fig. 118.*

Fig. 118 This Siwertell shiploader is totally enclosed for environment-friendly bulk handling

Shipping mark Markings distinctly displayed on goods being shipped, or on their packaging, which help with identification when stowing goods in a ship and when delivering the goods to their destination, and which provide handling instructions. For identification, the name and address of the consignee, the port or place of destination and a package number, if there is more than one, should be specified. Handling instructions, such as the one specifying which way up the item must be and the location of lifting points, are very often represented by symbols.

Ship's gear Crane(s) or derrick(s) fixed to the deck of a ship for loading and discharging cargo and/or stores and spares. It is used for cargo at ports where there are no shore cranes or where the shore cranes are inefficient or of inadequate lifting capacity.

Ship's sweat Condensation which occurs when a ship sails from a warm to a relatively cool climate. The temperature of the cargo drops at a slower rate than that of the ship's environment. Moisture condenses on the inner surfaces of the ship or shipping container and drips onto the cargo. To avoid damage to the cargo caused by ship's sweat, it is important for cargo to be dry when loaded into the ship and ventilation is favoured when meeting these climatic conditions.

Ship's tackle Ship's equipment, such as ropes and pulleys, used for lifting.

Ship-to-shore crane Shore crane in a container terminal used to load and discharge containers. Important information is the height, outreach and lifting capacity, which between them determine the size of containership which can be handled.

Shore A prop, normally made of timber, placed at an angle against a cargo to support it and prevent it from moving. Shores may be used on the deck of the ship or inside a shipping container. To support a cargo in this way is to shore it.

Shore gear Cranes, situated on the quay, used for loading cargo to, or discharging cargo from, ships. Before a shipowner or charterer schedules or nominates a ship for a particular port, it is necessary to determine whether the port is equipped with cranes and that these are of sufficient capacity to lift the cargo, failing which, a ship that has lifting gear is required.

Short sea trader Ship used to carry goods internationally but over relatively short distances. This term is often used synonymously with the coaster which carries cargoes between ports on the same coast or between ports of the same country. There is no real distinction in terms of construction between the two; ships in either trade are of very varied type: they may have one deck or more than one deck, they may be geared or gearless, they may have one hatch or several, and may be fitted to carry shipping containers. As a rule, they are small in relation to ocean-going vessels.

Shrink-wrapping Method of packing goods involving wrapping them in a material, which is then heated so that it shrinks and holds the goods securely. *See Fig. 119.*

Side rail

Fig. 119 Shrink-wrapping

Shuttle tanker   Tanker which transports oil from offshore production and storage facilities to onshore terminals.

Side door   *See* **Side ramp**.

Side door container   Shipping container whose doors are on one or both sides rather than at the rear. These containers are used when access to rear doors for loading or discharging would be difficult, for example when they are carried on rail wagons.

Side guard   Sheet placed along the side of a stack of goods to protect it from contact damage, particularly from fork-lift trucks. Typically, it is made of fibreglass.

Side rail   Steel section running along the length of each edge of a shipping container giving it structural strength. A standard container has two top side rails and two bottom side rails.

Side ramp Ramp fitted to the side of a ship to enable goods to be wheeled on and off. Such ramps are found on ro-ro ships, in particular, pure car carriers (PCCs) and pure car and truck carriers (PCTCs). They are also found on ships carrying unitised goods, such as pallet ships: the pallets are carried on fork-lift trucks over the ramp and set down on elevators in the ship, which convey them to the appropriate deck. There they are picked up by further fork-lift trucks to be placed in position for the voyage. When raised, this ramp becomes a watertight door, referred to as a side door. *See Fig. 120*.

Fig. 120 Pure car and truck carrier, the Grand Benelux; it has a capacity of 4,300 cars; its side ramp is visible amidships

Side tank Tank situated on either side of the centre tank of a tanker, viewed longitudinally. Side tanks extend the entire depth of the cargo space and are either the same size as, or smaller than the centre tank.

Sidelift truck Type of fork-lift truck whose forks are located along one side. It is designed to be operated in narrow aisles where use of a frontlift truck is difficult or impossible. It may be fitted with a top-lift attachment for lifting shipping containers.

Sideloader   Type of fork-lift truck whose forks are at the side. Such trucks are designed to facilitate movement of long, wide or awkward loads. They are also useful in narrow aisles in warehouses.

Side-loading trailer   Trailer equipped with its own equipment to load and offload containers. The aim is to eliminate waiting time and crane hire costs. This equipment can also transfer containers to and from rail wagons. Also known as a **sideloader** or self-loading trailer.

Silo   Tower-like structure, often cylindrical, used for the storage of grain, cement, coffee, fertiliser and other bulk cargoes. Typically, it is fed from the top by elevator and emptied from the base by gravity. *See Fig. 54a.*

Single buoy mooring (SBM)   Buoy to which a large oil tanker moors to discharge its cargo, which is then pumped by pipeline to a refinery. This facility avoids the need for a deep water terminal capable of handling such large vessels. Sometimes known as a **single-point buoy mooring**.

Single deck ship or single decker (SD)   Ship with one deck, that is, with no horizontal divisions within the hold or holds. An example of a single decker is a bulk carrier.

Single hatch vessel   Dry cargo ship whose hatchway is not divided lengthways (in contrast to a twin hatch vessel). It is especially suited to long length, awkwardly shaped cargoes.

Single sling   Sling, often made of rope or nylon, with an eye at each end, used for lifting a variety of types of cargo. Normally, one eye is placed on the hook of the crane, and the other on a running hook, that is, a hook that runs along the sling and tightens up round the piece of cargo.

Sister beam   Steel section which stretches along the length of a hatchway onto which the centre portions of boards, known as hatch boards, are placed to close the hatchway (the ends of the boards rest on king beams). This arrangement is used on older vessels and has largely been replaced by steel hatch covers.

Skeletal trailer   Road trailer that has no bed to carry a load but merely a framework onto which a shipping container is secured. *See Fig. 121.*

Skid

Fig. 121 Skeletal trailer

Skid One of the several pieces of wood attached to the underside of a heavy package to facilitate mechanical handling.

Skip Rectangular platform used to load and discharge small boxes of fragile and other miscellaneous small cargo. It has shallow iron fittings on the top and one open end.

Slave trailer Road trailer used in the operation of ro-ro vessels to transfer general cargo between the ship and shore.

Slewing crane Crane whose jib can be swung to one side or the other.

Slewing ramp Ramp, fitted to a ro-ro ship, which can be slewed or swung in such a way that it can connect to the shore in one of three directions: directly astern, from the port quarter or starboard quarter. This gives the ship greater flexibility of berthing positions and allows it to load or unload wheeled cargo at a variety of locations with or without port facilities. A semi-slewing ramp is a ramp which operates over one quarter only, either port or starboard, and can be slewed from a position directly astern to the angled position, port or starboard, as the case may be.

Sliding hatch cover   Type of hatch cover found on tween decks. It consists of a number of panels that slide one under the other when stowed. A large hatch might have two sets of panels that slide back to each end of the hatch when opened. This hatch cover is found on refrigerated ships, conventional general cargo ships and containerships. *See Fig. 122.*

Fig. 122 Sliding hatch covers

Sling   Piece of rope, canvas, polyester or chain links. Its ends have rings that are joined together so that it forms a loop which is slung around cargoes in bags and bales, for example, so that these can be lifted. Normally, slings are removed from the cargo after the lift has been completed, but in some cases they are left in position after loading and during transit so as to simplify and speed up discharging. *For examples, see* **Canvas sling, Chain sling, Rope sling** *and* **Wire sling**. *See Figs. 13, 15, 22, 82, 123, 129, 141, 148.*

Slop tank

Fig. 123 Chain slings

Slop tank Tank in a tanker into which slops are pumped. These represent a residue of the ship's cargo of oil together with the water used to clean the cargo tanks. They are left to separate out in the slop tank.

Slops Residue of a ship's cargo of oil together with the water used to clean the cargo tanks.

Slot Compartment in the hold of a containership into which a shipping container fits exactly. It is used in preference to the alternative term 'cell' when referring to the number of such compartments on a ship and the arrangements sometimes made between different shipping lines to pool capacity or between a shipping line and a groupage operator or non-vessel operating carrier (NVOC) to make use of space on the ship.

Smart seal *See* **Electronic seal**.

Snatch block Long, flat pulley whose block is open on one side, so as to insert easily a double wire or rope.

Snotter Type of sling made of rope or wire. An eye is formed at either end of a straight length for attaching to a hook for lifting.

Socket Point of a ship's electrical supply to which a refrigerated container is connected.

Space filler   Paperboard honeycomb used to fill crosswise spaces between goods in shipping containers, trucks or rail wagons. This is to avoid shifting or toppling of goods while in transit. Also known as a void filler.

Spar ceiling   *See* **Cargo battens**.

Specific gravity   Ratio of the weight of a liquid to its cubic capacity.

Spillage   Small quantities of a bulk cargo lost overboard during loading or discharge of a ship when using grabs.

Spiral elevator   Unloading equipment at a port which receives bagged, cased or palletised goods from a ship and lifts them, winding round as they rise, inside a tower to a conveyor which carries them to a warehouse. This method minimises unloading time and allows cargo operations to be carried out in all weathers.

Spiral shiploader   Equipment at a port which receives bagged goods from a warehouse, lowers them, winding round as they are lowered, inside a tower after which they are conveyed to the ship. This method increases the loading rate of the ship and allows cargo operations to be carried out in all weathers.

Spout   Pipe which projects beyond the quay and over the hatchway of a ship and directs bulk cargoes such as grain into the holds. A bulk cargo which is levelled in the hold or holds of a ship simply by moving the spout to and fro is said to be **spout trimmed**. Spouts may be telescopic to assist with different height requirements. *See Figs.* **5**, **75**.

Spreader beam   Device usually made of steel, which is attached to a crane for lifting awkwardly shaped or long length pieces of cargo and for handling shipping containers. Spreader beams, or simply **spreaders,** for general cargo may consist of a single steel bar; these allow cargo to be lifted more safely and efficiently and, important with some cargoes, lifted without bending or flexing. The sort of spreader beam used for handling containers may be of various types, all of which are solid pieces of equipment which fit onto the corner castings of the container. Spreader beams may be of fixed length and in various sizes to accommodate the different standard container lengths or may be telescopic, capable of manual or automatic adjustment to fit the container. Spreader beams are used as attachments not only to quay cranes and deck cranes but also to other lifting devices such as straddle carriers. They may be hydraulically driven, or electric, or a combination of both. *See Figs.* **10b**, *29,* **34a, 34b, 60, 79, 124a, 124b, 124c,** *129, 140.*

Spreader beam

Fig. 124a Spreaders; the left-hand one has a lifting capacity of 25 tonnes, the right-hand one, 30 tonnes. Both are 6 metres in length

Fig. 124b Semi-automatic spreader; hooking (attaching the crane's hook) is automatic, unhooking is manual. It has a 70-tonne lifting capacity

Fig. 124c A 50-tonne spreader

Stacking hatch cover

Square of the hatch Area of a ship's hold directly underneath the hatchway and occupying the same area. Certain goods require to be stowed in this space so that they can be loaded and discharged without being moved into and out of the wings of the ship; this reduces the possibility of handling damage.

Squat (to) Said of a ship, to increase draught as the speed is reduced.

Squeeze clamps Clamps, two of which are fitted to a fork-lift truck replacing the forks. They are used to grip the sides of unit loads or large bales. *See Fig. 125*.

Fig. 125 Squeeze clamps

Stackable flat Flatrack which, when empty, may be interlocked with other similar empty flatracks into a stack which has the same dimensions as a single standard shipping container, enabling them to be transported in the same way. Flats that are stackable in this way are known as collapsible flatracks when they have corner posts, which are collapsed when not in use, and folding flatracks when they have ends that are folded down. Both types are designed for the carriage of cargoes of awkward size.

Stacker crane Crane which may be on wheels or on tracks, capable of lifting shipping containers within its own framework. It is used in the same way as a **straddle carrier** in container terminals and depots but can also be rail-mounted. Also known as a straddle crane.

Stacking cone *See* **Cone**.

Stacking hatch cover Hatch cover consisting of several panels which are stacked one on top of another when opened. This is achieved by lifting, electrically or hydraulically, the first panel and sliding the next one underneath.

Stanchion

The resulting stack is then lifted higher so that each successive panel can be rolled underneath. The stack is positioned either in the hatchway itself at one end or just beyond the end of the hatchway. This type of hatch cover is used on weather decks and tween decks and is suitable for multi-purpose and general cargo ships.

Stanchion Upright used as a structural support. An example is the type of pillar in the hold of a ship that supports a deck.

Staple U-shaped fitting fixed inside a shipping container, several of which are located along the top and bottom corners. They are used for securing cargo. Staples that are applied with a stapler are also used to secure straps to flat rail wagons.

Starboard or **starboard side** The right side of a ship when viewed facing forwards.

Stay Rope or wire used to support a mast or a derrick, secured at one end to the mast and, at the other, to the deck. With main masts and heavy derricks several stays are set up, namely back stays, fore stays and topmast stays.

Steam guy One of a pair of wires or ropes fitted on either side of a ship's derrick between the derrick head and a winch on the deck. It is used to pull the derrick into the desired positions when working a heavy lift.

Steel Product which has many forms, and these may be categorised in various ways. Steel is either finished or semi-finished. Semi-finished products, such as billets, blooms and slabs, require further processing before they become finished products. Such processing may involve coating, shotblasting and priming, or drawing. It is normally possible to store semi-finished products in the open. Finished products need to be protected against the elements and are generally stored in covered warehouses. Depending on the product and the quantity, steel products are carried conventionally, often in bulk carriers or smaller single deck vessels, or sometimes in containers.

Steel billets, blooms and slabs Semi-finished steel products, otherwise termed semis, produced in different sizes and used for re-rolling into a variety of products. *See* **Steel**.

Steel coils Product carried in large quantities around the world and used in many industries including car bodies and parts and white goods. Coils are shipped in two basic forms: hot rolled and coated. In hot-rolled form, they are unpacked and require little or no protection against the elements, other than

Steel coils

against salt water, since they will be further processed prior to their end use. Coated steel is normally packed in an outer envelope, normally of metal, and may have further protection against humidity. Narrow strip is a variation which is used for a wide variety of applications. *See* **Steel**. *See Figs. 26, 48a, 48b, 49b,* ***126a, 126b***.

Fig. 126a Steel coils. These are wrapped for protection

Fig. 126b Attachment to a fork-lift truck for steel coils. These are teflon-coated to avoid damage to the inside of coils

Steel pipes

Steel pipes Long hollow steel products used widely in the oil and water industries. They may be supplied and shipped uncoated (bare) or coated inside or outside in different ways, such as with concrete, which acts as a corrosion resistant. Coated pipes require careful handling to avoid damage to the coating. They are shipped loose or in bundles. Often used interchangeably with steel tubes. *See* **Steel**. *See Figs.* ***127****, 140*.

Fig. 127 Coated pipes on a rail wagon; note the wood separating the pipes to avoid damage

Steel plates Steel product which has many purposes including flooring, boilers and earth-moving equipment. They are shipped loose or in bundles, depending on their individual weight. *See* **Steel**. *See Figs. 94a,* ***128***.

Fig. 128 Steel plates

Steel rails Steel products for railways and bridges; they are shipped loose or in bundles and are being manufactured in increasingly long lengths, which reduces the amount of track welding required. Long lengths require the use of spreaders when being handled. *See* **Steel**. *See Figs. 101, **129**.*

Fig. 129 Steel rails being loaded; from the top, note the spreader, the chain slings and straps. The ship's hatch covers are folded back to allow access to the hold

Steel sheet piling Steel product that is used in construction, for example to provide a surrounding wall for basements or walls for docks. They may be shipped loose or in bundles and have two basic profiles: Z-shaped and u-shaped. *See* **Steel**. *See Fig. 130.*

Steel piling

Fig. 130 Steel sheet piling; this type is known as Z-shaped, or Frodingham, piling; note the timber separations allowing a small number of bars to be lifted

Steel piling   *See* **Steel sheet piling**.

Steel strip   Steel product with various end uses. It is produced in coils of various weights and dimensions. *See* **Steel**. *See Figs. 81, 126a.*

Steel tubes   *See* **Steel pipes**.

Steel universal beams and columns   Steel product which is used widely as a framework for buildings. They consist of two flanges connected by a web, making an 'H' (columns) or 'I' (beams) shape. They may be shipped loose or in bundles. *See* **Steel**. *See Fig. 75.*

Stem   Forward-most part of a ship at the point where the ship's sides meet at the bows.

Stern   The rear of the ship. Also known as the after end.

Stern door Door at the stern or rear of a ro-ro ship. It is situated forward of the ramp and provides a watertight barrier against the entry of seawater.

Stern ramp Inclined plane which connects the after end of a ro-ro ship with the shore or quay on which rolling cargo is wheeled or driven onto and off the ship. The ramp is very often designed to make a watertight door to cover the opening in the ship. *See Fig. 131.*

Fig. 131 Stern ramp

Stevedore Person running a business whose functions are to load, stow and discharge ships. Often used synonymously with docker.

Stevedore's hook Curved piece of steel with a point, held in the hand by a docker, used to attach to sacks of cargo for the purpose of moving them from place to place, both on shore and in the hold of a ship. Also known as a docker's hook or hand hook (as distinct from a cargo hook, which is attached to a crane or derrick).

Stiff Said of a ship, having a tendency to roll quickly due to a large metacentric height often caused by stowing dense cargoes low in a ship.

Stiffeners

Stiffeners Bags of grain stowed on top of bulk grain in a ship's holds. Their purpose is to prevent the bulk cargo from shifting with the rolling and pitching of the ship. When the grain is discharged, these bags are usually cut and the grain is incorporated into the bulk.

Sto-ro System of stowing cargo conventionally on a ro-ro ship. The cargo is wheeled on and off the ship on trailers of various sorts, depending on the particular circumstances, but is removed from the trailers and stowed directly on the deck or tank top for the duration of the voyage.

Stopper Short rope or chain, of which there are many types, used to check the running of cables.

Stowage The placing of goods in a ship in such a way as to ensure, first, the safety and stability of the ship not only on a sea or ocean passage but also in between ports when parts of the cargo have been loaded or discharged, as the case may be; secondly, the safety of the individual consignments, which should not be damaged or contaminated by being in proximity to goods with which they are not compatible; thirdly, the ability to unload goods at their port of discharge without having to move goods destined for other ports. **To stow** goods is to arrange or position them in a ship for their carriage to the port of discharge.

Stowage factor Ratio of a cargo's cubic measurement to its weight, expressed in cubic feet to the ton or cubic metres to the tonne. The stowage factor is used in conjunction with a ship's grain capacity or bale capacity, depending on the properties of the cargo, to determine the total quantity of cargo that can be loaded.

Stowage plan Plan, in the form of a longitudinal cross-section of a ship, which shows where in the ship all the consignments are stowed. It is frequently colour-coded to highlight the different ports of discharge. The stowage plan is often sent to the stevedores at each of the discharge ports to assist them in planning the discharging of the ship.

Stowing ramp Type of internal ramp inside a ro-ro ship which connects one deck with another. It can be secured in the elevated position to allow greater headroom for larger vehicles.

Straddle carrier Wheeled vehicle designed to lift and carry shipping containers within its own framework. It is used for moving, and sometimes stacking, containers at a container terminal. *See Fig. 132.*

Strengthened hold

Fig. 132 Straddle carrier

Straddle crane Crane, on wheels or tracks, which can lift shipping containers within its own framework. It is used in the same way as a straddle carrier in container terminals and depots but can also be rail-mounted. Also known as a **stacker crane**.

Strap Means of securing cargo when on a ship, vehicle, trailer, rail wagon or pallet. Straps generally have a type of buckle that permits them to tighten up to a stated breaking strength, which is measured in kilogrammes or tonnes.

Strap seal *See* **Strip seal**.

Strapping Practice of securing holds partly filled with grain by lashing or strapping timber over the surface of the cargo. This is to prevent the shifting of the cargo.

Strengthened hold Hold of a ship whose tank top is reinforced so as to be able to carry dense cargoes such as ore.

String of barges Group of barges tied together for towing. Also referred to as a train of barges. *See Fig. 133.*

Fig. 133 String of barges

Stringer or **stringer plate** Steel plate used to stiffen the interior of a ship's plating. It is sometimes a requirement in charter-parties that cargo be dunnaged so as to prevent contact with the ship's stringers.

Strip seal Indicative type of seal, intended to show, when damaged, that unauthorised access has been made to a shipping container. It consists of a strip of metal or plastic attached to the rods or arms on the doors of a shipping container, looped through a hole in the rod and secured by being tightened through a ratchet device. It is removed by cutting and is subsequently not reusable. Sometimes referred to as a strap seal.

Strip (to) To unload a shipping container. Also known as to destuff.

Stripping pump Pump in a tanker which is brought into use towards completion of discharge to drain the tanks of their remaining cargo. Steam driven or electrically driven, it pumps at a considerably slower rate than the main pumps.

Stuff (to) To load a shipping container.

Suction elevator Method of unloading grain cargoes from ships using a vacuum to obtain pneumatic suction. The cargo is sucked up through pipes.

Suezmax Maximum size of a ship of certain categories, capable of transiting the Suez Canal. The most common is the **Suezmax tanker** of 120,000–200,000 tonnes deadweight. The **Suezmax containership** has a container capacity of about 12,000 TEUs.

Sugar Foodstuff derived either from sugar cane or sugar beet, it is transported in bulk and in bags. The final, processed, product is transported in bulk and carried by road in dry bulk road tankers, by rail in tank wagons, and by sea in bulk carriers. It may also be transported from door to door in bulk containers. When in bags, it is transported conventionally or in general purpose containers. Bags may be of the smaller type, typically 50kg, and made of paper or fibre, or bulk bags of various sizes (*see* **Bulk bag**). At the loading port, sugar is kept under cover in warehouses prior to shipment. *See also* **Bulk carrier** *and* **Bulk container**.

Sulphuric acid carrier Tanker specially equipped to carry sulphuric acid. Because of the highly corrosive nature of this product, the cargo tanks are lined with one of a variety of linings or coatings. Heating coils are necessary to maintain the correct temperature. Sulphuric acid gives off noxious gases, which have to be vented away safely.

Summer deadweight Quantity which a ship can carry when loaded to its summer load line.

Summer draught Depth of water to which a ship's hull may be immersed in a summer zone at all times or in a seasonal zone at certain times of the year. The depth is indicated by the summer load line painted on the ship's sides.

Summer freeboard Distance between the deck line of a ship and its summer load line.

Summer load line Line painted on the sides of a ship, which shows the maximum depth to which that ship's hull may be immersed when in a summer zone. The line is marked with an 'S'. Also referred to as the Plimsoll Line or the ship's **summer marks**.

Summer tank Tank in a type of tanker known as a summer tank ship. Void spaces on either side of the tank are enclosed so as to form additional tanks

Summer timber freeboard

which allow more cargo to be carried when the vessel is sailing in a summer load line zone. These tanks would be left empty when in a winter zone.

Summer timber freeboard Distance between the deck line of a ship and its summer timber load line.

Summer timber load line Line painted on the sides of a ship which shows the maximum depth to which that ship's hull may be immersed when in a summer zone with a deck cargo of timber.

Summer zone One of the several geographical areas defined by the International Conference on Load Lines, where a ship's hull may be immersed no deeper than its summer load line.

Super-rack Proprietary type of flatrack with telescopic end posts whose height can be adjusted to accommodate overheight cargo. *See Figs. **134a**, **134b***.

Fig. 134a Side view of a stack of super-racks

Swapbody

Fig. 134b End view of a super-rack showing capacities

Superpack   Bundle of aluminium ingots weighing 25 tonnes. *See Fig. 2c.*

Super-Post-Panamax containership   *See* **Post-Panamax (ship)**.

Super-Post-Panamax crane   *See* **Post-Panamax crane**.

Supply-ship   Ship used in the offshore drilling industry. As well as carrying out the normal duties of delivering supplies, its duties include towing (when it is sometimes termed a tug/supply-ship), anchor handling, survey work and rescue work.

Support ship   Vessel used in the offshore industry for testing and servicing undersea construction work. Typically it has its own cranes, diving bells, a helicopter deck, and possibly photographic and research laboratories. If engaged in diving support, it might have compression chambers.

Swapbody   Type of trailer used for combined rail and road transport. As its name suggests, it is adaptable to being towed by a tractor unit on the roads as well as being carried on rail wagons. It was designed to maximise the number of pallets carried and, at 2.5 metres wide, it is wider than a standard shipping container. It has four legs on which it stands to enable a tractor unit to be placed underneath it. Early designs had soft tops and were incapable of being stacked but more recently many different models have appeared including hard-top versions. These can be stacked whether empty or loaded. Also spelled **swap body** or **swopbody or swop body**.

Sweat Condensation which occurs when a ship sails either from a cool to a relatively warm climate (*see* **Cargo sweat**) or from a warm to a relatively cool climate (*see* **Ship's sweat**). Often, the expert use of ventilation is required to prevent sweat which can cause serious damage to cargoes.

Sweep the holds (to) To clear away, from the holds of a ship, rubbish or leakage from bags or cases, after a cargo has been discharged so that the holds are clean in readiness for the next cargo. It is often a requirement of time charter-parties that the holds of the ship be clean or swept clean on delivery to the time charterer at the beginning of the period of the charter and, similarly, on re-delivery to the shipowner at the end of the charter. Such rubbish or leakage is known as **sweepings**.

Swinging buoy Mooring buoy used by a tanker which allows it to swing with the tide.

Swinging derrick Term given to a derrick which is used on its own in a similar way to a crane. Whereas derricks are often used in pairs (union purchase), these are fixed; a swinging derrick can slew or swing, thus making it easier to spot (place) the cargo in the desired place on board or ashore. Cargo is attached to the hook, lifted by pulling on the fall and slewed or swung by means of winches.

Tackle Collection of wires and ropes used with a ship's derrick to lift goods. Also used to describe the method of rigging a derrick consisting of two blocks with a rope or wire passing through them in a particular configuration.

Taint Trace of a substance found in a cargo which contaminates that cargo and is likely to make it unfit for its original purpose. Some cargoes, like citrus fruit, have a tendency to taint others while some, like tea, are more susceptible than others to being tainted themselves.

Tandem Two cranes are said to be worked **in tandem** when they are employed together so as to make use of their combined lifting capacity when handling lifts in excess of their individual capacities.

Tank barge River barge designed for the carriage of liquid bulk cargoes.

Tank car Type of container used for conveying liquids in bulk by rail.

Tank cleaning Removal of all traces of a cargo from the tanks of a tanker normally by means of high-pressure water jets. Tanks are cleaned to avoid contamination and, where applicable, to remove toxic or explosive gases that might remain after a cargo has been discharged.

Tank container Shipping container designed for the carriage of liquids. It consists of a cylindrical tank made of stainless steel surrounded by a framework which gives it the same overall dimensions as those of a standard dry cargo container, enabling it to be carried and handled in the same way. Products carried in tank containers range from potable spirits, such as whisky, to hazardous chemicals. *See Fig. 135.*

Fig. 135 Tank containers showing how their frames enable them to be stacked in the same way as ordinary shipping containers

Tank terminal

Tank terminal or **tank farm** Facility at a port where liquid cargoes are received, stored and distributed. These are stored in tanks of various sizes, some of which may be coated inside or made of stainless steel and some heated with heating coils or insulated. Processing facilities, such as blending, filtering and loading into drums, may also be available. Products stored include fuel oils, vegetable oils and chemicals.

Tank top Floor of the hold of a ship, so called because it forms the top of the double-bottom tank. It is important to know the strength of the tank top, especially when loading dense cargoes. This is expressed in tonnes per square metre and represents the maximum weight that can be loaded onto it. This limitation is calculated by the ship's classification society. Also spelled **tank-top**.

Tanker Ship designed for the carriage of liquid in bulk, its cargo space consisting of several, or indeed many, tanks. Tankers carry a wide variety of products including crude oil, refined products, liquid gas and wine. Size and capacity range from the ultra-large crude carrier (ULCC) of over half a million tonnes to the small coastal tanker of a few hundred tonnes. Tankers load their cargo by gravity from the shore or by shore pumps and discharge using their own pumps.

Tare or **tare weight** Weight of wrapping or packing. This is added to the net weight of a cargo to determine its gross weight. In the case of shipping containers, the tare represents the weight of the container without its contents.

Tarpaulin Waterproof canvas sheet used to protect goods from, for example, rain and sea water. Tarpaulins are used in a variety of situations: for example, to cover goods on lorries or on the ground when goods are stowed out of doors. They cover open-top containers and prevent water entering while giving a measure of protection against condensation. They are also used together with hatch boards to cover hatch openings on older vessels.

Telescopic spreader Device usually made of steel which is attached to a crane for handling shipping containers. It is one of a variety of spreader beams used for handling containers, all of which are solid pieces of equipment that fit onto the corner castings of the container. The telescopic version is capable of manual or automatic adjustment to fit the container. *See Figs. 136, 140.*

Fig. 136 Reach stacker with telescopic spreader lifting a steel pipe

Temperature recorder Device which measures and records the temperature over a period of time within an insulated shipping container. Such a device may also be combined with a hygrometer and used in the hold of a ship to record not only temperature but also humidity.

Tender Said of a ship, unstable due to having a small metacentric height, which gives a tendency to roll slowly. This condition is often caused by stowing dense cargoes too high in the ship.

Tensioner Device which applies tension to wires or ropes, for example, when bundling goods together. Tensioners are of two basic types, manual and pneumatic.

Terminal chassis Trailer which is only used within a terminal, such as a port terminal, to transport loads between the ship and the warehouse. It is attached to a tractor for this purpose.

Terminal tractor Vehicle which is only used within a terminal to pull trailers. *See Fig. 137.*

Fig. 137 Terminal tractor pulling trailers with containers

Threefold purchase Method of rigging a derrick using two threefold blocks, the lower one carrying the hook and having the rope or wire in six parts. The gain in power, known as the purchase, is roughly equivalent to the number of parts of the rope, in this case by a factor of six. The safe working load of the derrick should nevertheless not be exceeded. Also known as treble purchase.

Thrower Machine used in trimming dry bulk cargo in a ship's hold. The bulk is fed through an overhead hopper to the thrower which projects it in a stream into the wings. It can be used in either the lower hold or the tween deck. A centrifugal thrower has a jet which revolves through 360 degrees so that the stream of bulk cargo is distributed in all directions. This machine is

Timber deck cargo

used for stowing sugar, ores and minerals in the holds of bulk carriers or in warehouses.

Tier limit or **tier limitation** Maximum number of levels of a commodity which may be stowed on top of each other without suffering damage from compression.

Timber carrier Ship designed for the carriage of timber, usually geared and having large hatchways. Sometimes referred to as a forest products carrier.

Timber deck cargo Practice of carrying timber cargoes not only in the holds of ships but also on the deck because of its high stowage factor. Because of the height of the cargo, strict regulations exist which call for a compact stow and secure lashing. *See Fig. 138.*

Fig. 138 Timber deck cargo

Timber dogs

Timber dogs Pair of metal hooks, linked together with a chain, used for lifting large timber logs. The hooks have sharp points that penetrate the timber when lifted. In common with other lifting devices, timber dogs have a safe working load, which must not be exceeded.

Timber freeboard The distance between the deck line, that is, the line representing the uppermost continuous deck, and the relevant timber load line, painted on the side of the ship. Freeboards are assigned by a government department or, if authorised by that department, a classification society.

Timber load line One of the lines painted on the sides of a ship, which show the maximum depths to which that ship's hull may be immersed when arriving at, sailing through or putting to sea in the different load line zones with a deck cargo of timber. The positioning of these lines is determined by the rules agreed at the International Conference on Load Lines, which have been ratified by many maritime countries. Also known as the lumber load line.

Timber, packaged *See* **Packaged timber**.

Tine (of a coil hook) Horizontal prong on a coil hook which is inserted in the bore of a steel coil to lift it.

Tipping hatch *See* **Bulk discharge open-top container**. *See Figs. 71, 139*.

Fig. 139 Rear view of a bulk container showing the tipping hatch

Tobacco terminal Terminal in a port dedicated to the handling and storage of tobacco. As tobacco is affected by moisture, storage sheds require dehumidifying equipment and good ventilation. Lighting in the warehouse must also be neutral since tobacco is assessed primarily on its colour.

Tomming or **tomming down** Bracing of cargo in a ship with timber under deck beams and on a plank to hold down cases, bales and some other types of cargo. The purpose is to prevent the cargo from shifting.

Tongs Implement having a scissor action used for handling and lifting certain commodities. In the case of timber, tongs are used for separating logs. They are also used, when attached to a chain, for lifting, for example, rails.

Tonnage (1) Quantity of cargo, normally expressed as a number of tonnes or tons.

Tonnage (2) Cubic capacity of a ship. *See* **Net tonnage (NT)** *and* **Gross tonnage (GT)**.

Tonnage (3) Cargo capacity of all the ships of a country or of a particular trade, depending on the context in which it is used.

Tonnage mark Mark painted on the side of a shelter-deck ship which, depending on whether it is submerged or not, determines whether the ship's larger or smaller register tonnage applies when port dues are assessed for a particular voyage.

Tonnage opening Permanent opening in the shelter-deck of a ship, which is designed such that her registered tonnage would not include the shelter-deck space, although this space is capable of carrying cargo. *See also* **Shelter-deck ship**.

Tonnes per centimetre (TPC) Quantity of cargo needed to immerse a ship one further centimetre. It is found in the ship's deadweight scale, a table which also shows in columns a set of draughts with the ship's corresponding deadweight tonnages when it is lying in salt water and fresh water. The quantity varies not only ship by ship but also according to the quantity already on board. It may alternatively be expressed in (long) **tons per inch (TPI)**.

Top off (to) To fill a ship that is already partly loaded with cargo. This operation occurs when there is a draught limitation at the first load port or between there and the open sea, such as a sand bar. The ship loads a quantity of cargo

Top pick

corresponding to the permissible draught, then fills up at the second port where there is no restriction.

Top pick   *See* **Container handler**.

Top side rail   Steel section running along the length of each top edge of a shipping container giving it structural strength.

Top stow cargo   Goods which are stowed on top of all others in a ship's hold because of their relatively low density and the probability that they would be damaged if overstowed. By definition, goods placed at the top of the cargo because they are for discharge at the next port of call are also termed top stow cargo.

Toplift or **toplift attachment**   Attachment to a fork-lift truck, designed to lift a shipping container. It sits across the top of the container and is secured by twist locks at the top corners of the container. *See Fig. 140*.

Fig. 140 Fork-lift truck with a toplift attachment equipped with a telescopic spreader

Topside tank Upper wing tank of a bulk carrier, which is used either for cargo or for ballast.

Total deadweight (TDW) Difference between a ship's loaded and light displacements, consisting of the total weight of cargo, fuel, fresh water, stores and crew, which a ship can carry when immersed to a particular load line, normally its summer load line. The deadweight is expressed in tons or tonnes. Also referred to as deadweight or deadweight all told.

Tractor Self-propelled vehicle used for towing trailers. In ports, tractors may be used to move terminal trailers or road trailers onto and off ro-ro ships. *See Figs. 29, 137.*

Trailer Vehicle on which goods are loaded and towed by a tractor.

Trailer deck Deck on a ro-ro vessel dedicated to the stowage of road trailers. It is similar to a car deck but has a higher clearance.

Train ferry Ship designed to carry rail wagons. These may be cargo wagons or passenger cars. The wagons are shunted onto train decks, which have tracks laid on them. There are various configurations possible which determine the number of tracks. Pure train ferries carry only rail traffic while vehicle/train ferries, alternatively known as train/vehicle ferries, carry road vehicles as well. As an example, a vehicle/train ferry might have a railway track in the middle of the deck with two lines of road vehicles, one on either side.

Train of barges Group of barges tied together for towing. Also referred to as a string of barges.

Tramp or **tramp ship** Ship that will call at any port to carry whatever cargoes are available, normally on the basis of a charter or part charter. Such a ship is the opposite of a liner ship which trades on a specific route between advertised ports.

Transhipment Transfer of goods from one vessel to another. This transfer may be direct or it may be necessary to discharge the goods onto the quay prior to loading them onto the second vessel, or onto a vehicle should the second vessel be loading at a different berth. Alternative spellings are **trans-shipment** and **transshipment**.

Transit cargo Goods which are discharged from a sea-going ship in one country but which are destined for another country.

Translifter Type of tractor used for towing roll trailers and cassettes. In the case of cassettes, it raises and provides axles and wheels for both ends. It serves the same purpose for the wheelless end of a roll trailer.

Transloader Vessel or barge used to transfer cargo from one ship to another. Often conversions, these ships are self-discharging. Depending on the type of cargo to be transferred, these vessels may be equipped with cranes or conveyors.

Transporter crane Type of crane used for handling shipping containers. Typically, it is a rope-hoisting, rope-traversing crane that operates by lifting the container (hoisting) and moving it along a trolley (traversing) before lowering it into position. The crane moves along the length of the quay on rails. It is equipped with a spreader beam which attaches to the corner castings of the container to enable it to be lifted.

Transtainer Range of proprietary container gantry cranes used to move and stack containers in a container yard. They may be rubber-tyred or railmounted.

Travelling gantry crane *See* **Gantry crane**. *See Fig. 50.*

Tray Rectangular wooden platform used to carry cases and cartons containing such goods as fruit when being loaded onto and discharged from a ship.

Treble purchase Method of rigging a derrick using two threefold blocks, the lower one carrying the hook and having the rope or wire in six parts. The gain in power, known as the purchase, is roughly equivalent to the number of parts of the rope, in this case by a factor of six. The safe working load of the derrick should nevertheless not be exceeded. Also known as threefold purchase.

Trim Relationship between a ship's draughts forward and aft. Consideration is given to the trim when loading cargo since it is desirable to sail with a reasonably even keel. Failing this, a ship is safer down by the stern, that is, with the draught aft slightly deeper than the draught forward. In this condition, it is said to be **trimmed by the stern**. Adjustments can be made to the trim by the way in which the cargo is distributed in the hold or holds and by means of water ballast, for example, in the peak tanks. A ship is said to be **trimmed by the head** if its draught forward is slightly deeper than its draught aft. To adjust the draughts in this way is to trim a ship.

Trim cargo (to) To level a cargo in the hold of a ship to contribute to its stability at sea. This is done in different ways, depending on the cargo and the facilities; for example, a coal cargo may be spout trimmed, that is, made level while actually being loaded by the movement to and fro of the spout from which the cargo is poured into the ship; a grain cargo might be levelled by bulldozers moving across it after it is loaded.

Trimodal Relating to shipment by three modes of transport: water, rail and road. Also spelled **tri-modal.**

Tropical draught Depth of water to which a ship may be immersed in a tropical zone as indicated by the tropical load line painted on the side of the ship in accordance with the load line regulations.

Tropical freeboard Distance between the deck line of a ship and its tropical load line.

Tropical fresh water load line Line painted on the sides of a ship, which shows the maximum depth to which that ship's hull may be immersed when in fresh water in a tropical zone. The line is marked TF.

Tropical fresh water timber load line Line painted on the sides of a ship, which shows the maximum depth to which that ship's hull may be immersed when in fresh water in a tropical zone with a deck cargo of timber. The line is marked LTF.

Tropical load line Line painted on the sides of a ship, which shows the maximum depth to which that ship's hull may be immersed when in a tropical zone. The line is marked T.

Tropical timber freeboard Distance between the deck line of a ship and its tropical timber load line.

Tropical timber load line Line painted on the sides of a ship, which shows the maximum depth to which that ship's hull may be immersed when in a tropical zone with a deck cargo of timber. The line is marked LT.

Tropical zone One of several geographical areas, defined by the International Conference on Load Lines, where a ship's hull may be immersed no deeper than its tropical load line.

Truck sling Network of wire slings used in pairs to put under the axles of a truck to lift it. *See Fig. 141.*

Tug

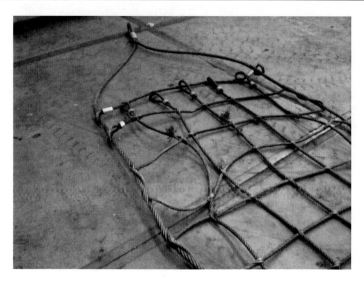

Fig. 141 Truck sling; two slings similar to the one illustrated are together capable of lifting 25 tonnes

Tug Small, powerful vessel used for towing or pushing ships in port, towing or pushing barges along rivers or towing, for example, oil rigs out to sea. Its ability to pull or push is called its bollard pull, which is expressed in tonnes. *See Fig. 133.*

Turnbuckle Device which applies tension to ropes or chains used for lashing cargo. Also referred to as a bottle screw. *See Fig. 142.*

Fig. 142 Turnbuckle

Tween deck Deck which separates the hold of a ship into two, making an upper hold and a lower hold. Its purpose is to provide two separate levels of stowage for the cargo, giving ease of access and helping to avoid compression of cargo caused by direct overstowage. The tween decks have hatch covers in the same way as the main deck but very often these are flush with the deck to enable vehicles and fork-lift trucks to move easily across them. It is important to know the strength of the tween deck and the tween deck hatch cover, especially when loading dense cargoes. These are expressed in tonnes per square metre and represent the maximum weight which can be loaded onto the tween deck and tween deck hatch cover, respectively. These limitations are calculated by the ship's classification society.

Tween deck vessel or **tween decker** Popular type of general cargo ship whose holds are divided horizontally by one or more decks, known as tween decks. This arrangement allows a wide range of commodities to be carried effectively and safely, normally by stowing heavier, denser cargoes in the lower hold and lighter cargoes in the upper part of the hold on the tween deck or decks. The tween decks have hatch covers in the same way as the main deck but very often these are flush with the deck to enable vehicles and fork-lift trucks to move easily across them. These vessels are of either the single hatch or twin hatch type: the single hatch version has hatchways whose breadth covers a good part of the beam of the vessel; the twin hatch version has hatchways divided lengthways to facilitate loading close to the ship's sides.

Twenty-foot equivalent unit (TEU) Unit of measurement equivalent to one 20-foot shipping container. Thus, one 40-foot container is equal to two TEUs. This measurement is used to quantify, for example, the container capacity of a ship, the number of containers carried on a particular voyage or over a period of time, or it may be the unit on which freight is payable.

Twin hatch vessel Dry cargo ship whose hatchways are divided lengthways into two halves. This enables cargo to be loaded and stowed nearer to the ship's sides without much, if any, extra handling.

Twist lock Device which is fitted into each of the four corner fittings of a shipping container and is turned or twisted, thus locking the container for the purpose of securing or lifting. On a flatrack, twist locks are used to hold the uprights in a vertical position and to lock several flats together when not being used for cargo so that they form one lift. Twist locks can be locked manually or automatically. Twist locks may be fitted to the decks of ships to secure containers to the deck. Some types have heads that retract below the deck level when not being used, to allow the deck to be used for non-containerised cargoes. Also spelled **twistlock**.

Two-way pallet Type of pallet in which the apertures intended to take the forks of a fork-lift truck are situated on two opposite edges. *See also* **Pallet**, **One-way pallet** *and* **Four-way pallet**.

ULCC *See* **Ultra-large crude carrier (ULCC)**.

Ullage Height of the space in a cargo tank or a tank container above the surface of the liquid cargo. This distance is used to calculate the volume of liquid in the tank or container. **Ullaging** is the measuring of this height by means of a tape inserted into the tank.

Ultra-large container ship (ULCS) New generation of containership being planned. She will have a container capacity of between 12,000 and 14,000 TEUs.

Ultra-large crude carrier (ULCC) Tanker of no official size but variously described as being anything between 350,000 tonnes deadweight and 550,000 tonnes deadweight.

Uncontainerable cargo or **uncontainerisable cargo** Cargo that, because of its overall dimensions, will not fit into or onto a single shipping container. On routes which are fully containerised, such cargo can sometimes be accommodated on two or more flatracks or platform flats. Cargo is also considered uncontainerable if it is too heavy for a single container. In this case, it may be secured on the deck of the ship. *See Fig. 143*.

Fig. 143 This example of uncontainerable cargo, which is also a heavy lift, is a power transformer being loaded onto a truck.

Unit load

Underkeel clearance Minimum distance between the bottom of a ship and the bed of a river or sea, required by some authorities as a safety margin because of unseen hazards or climatic changes in the depth of water. Also known as keel clearance.

UNIMOG Proprietary name for a versatile, diesel-powered vehicle, capable of running on road or rail to haul road trailers or rail wagons. It has road wheels with rubber tyres, and two axles which can be lowered onto rails as necessary. *See Fig. 144.*

Fig. 144 UNIMOG – this model is based in the Port of Antwerp, Belgium

Union purchase Popular method of combining two derricks for the purpose of loading cargo to a ship or discharging it. One derrick is positioned over the hatch and the other over the quay. The two falls are connected together to the cargo hook. Once the cargo has been lifted to the desired height, it is swung by pulling on the ropes of one derrick and releasing those of the other.

Unit load Method of presenting goods for shipment such that they are in lifts of uniform size or weight, for example goods shipped on pallets or preslung. This method simplifies the handling of the cargo and increases the rate

Universal bulk carrier (UBC)

of loading and discharging of ships since there will be fewer, and heavier, lifts. To group goods together in this way is to **unitise** them; the grouping is termed **unitisation.**

Universal bulk carrier (UBC)   Early bulk carrier, having a single deck and hoppered holds, designed to carry a wide range of bulk cargoes (but only one at a time). It has separate upper holds which could be used for ballast or for dense cargoes such as iron ore, while the main holds carry less dense bulk cargoes.

Unloader   Generic name for port apparatus employed to unload ships and barges carrying dry bulk cargoes. Unloaders are normally associated with a high rate of discharge. There are two main types of unloader: continuous and discontinuous. Continuous unloaders operate in an uninterrupted and normally automated way. Discontinuous unloaders require an operator, with cargo being discharged in a series of individual lifts. Both types of unloader may be fixed or mobile, the latter being slower but allowing flexibility at terminals and ports by being capable of being moved wherever required. Performance is measured in tonnes per hour (TPH). *See Figs.* ***145a, 145b.***

Fig. 145a Unloader. Siwertell ship unloaders offer record-beating capacities and are totally enclosed for environment-friendly bulk handling

Urea handling

Fig. 145b Mobile unloading system, suitable for a wide range of bulk cargoes, equipped with a covered conveyor to minimise dust. This Siwertell mobile ship unloader is the ideal solution when unloading is required in more than one spot

Unprotected Said of goods that are shipped without any protective packing.

Upper tween deck Space for carrying cargo situated below the main deck of a ship and above the deck that divides the upper hold.

Urea Material which, when used industrially, is a synthesised version of the waste product of many living organisms. It is shipped in large quantities annually in bulk carriers and is used mainly in the manufacture of fertilisers.

Urea handling Large quantities of bulk or bags may be shipped in bulk carriers; smaller quantities are carried in bulk containers when loose and in general purpose containers when in bags. Loading of bulk carriers is normally by conveyor leading to a spout. Discharge from the ship is normally by crane equipped with a grab into hoppers positioned above trucks or rail wagons or belt conveyor which takes it to an area away from the quay for stacking. Discharge port terminals may have bagging facilities. *See Fig. 146.*

Vacuum unloader

Fig. 146 A bulk carrier offloads urea at the Port of Portland's (Oregon, USA) Terminal 2

Vacuum unloader   *See* **Pneumatic unloader**.

Vehicle carrier   Ship designed to carry unaccompanied new vehicles such as cars, trucks, trailers and buses. Replacing the bulk carriers which were originally used to carry cars on the outward leg and bulk cargoes on the return leg, the vehicle carrier has ro-ro type ramps which give access to a number of decks, typically 12 or 13. Hoistable decks allow height adjustment, enabling taller vehicles to be accommodated.

Vehicle/train ferry   Ship designed to carry rail wagons and road vehicles at the same time. Various configurations are possible, one being that rail wagons, which might be cargo wagons or passenger carriages, are shunted onto a central track with two lines of road vehicles, one on each side.

Ventilated container   Shipping container which resembles a general purpose container but which is designed to provide continuous ventilation for cargoes requiring it, in particular coffee. This is achieved by a series of holes along the top and bottom side rails of the container which provide ventilation throughout.

Ventilation The introduction of fresh air into the hold of a ship. The purpose is to warm or cool the cargo so as to prevent large differences occurring between the temperature of the cargo and that of the ship's environment, which would give rise to condensation. Ventilation is effected by means of ventilators of various types attached to the deck of the ship, or in fine weather by opening the hatches, or by a mechanical system which forces air into the hold. Ventilation is also used in certain types of shipping container.

Ventilator Duct attached to the deck of a ship which allows fresh air to enter the hold. Ventilators are of various types, the most common of which is the cowl type which can be swivelled to vary the rate of air flow into as well as out of the hold.

Very large containership Containership with a capacity of over 7,500 TEUs.

Very large crude carrier (VLCC) Large tanker of no official size but variously described as being anything between 100,000 tonnes deadweight and 350,000 tonnes deadweight.

Very large gas carrier (VLGC) LPG carrier in the range 70,000 to 86,000 cubic metre capacity class. These ships are also able to trade clean petroleum products such as naphtha.

Very large ore carrier (VLOC) Largest of the bulk carriers, of no official size, but often described as being of 250,000 tonnes deadweight or above.

Visor Opening at the forward end of a ferry which consists of the entire bow section. It is raised and held out of the way in port to allow the ramp to be accessed and vehicles to be driven on and off the ship. Normally the ramp itself is a watertight door so the visor does not have to fulfil this objective.

Void filler Paperboard honeycomb used to fill crosswise spaces between goods in shipping containers, trucks or rail wagons. This is to avoid shifting or toppling of goods while in transit. Also known as a space filler.

Warp (to) To shift a ship by means of its mooring ropes.

Water density Ratio of the weight of water to its volume. This ranges from 1,000 kilogrammes per cubic metre for fresh water to 1,026 kilogrammes for seawater, with brackish water in between. Seawater provides greater buoyancy than fresh water so a ship that has loaded in fresh water to its fresh water load line will rise to its summer load line by the time it reaches the open sea.

Weather deck

Weather deck Uppermost deck exposed to the weather, extending the length of the ship. It is important to know the strength of the weather deck, especially when loading dense cargoes on it. This is expressed in tonnes per square metre and represents the maximum weight which can be loaded onto the weather deck. This limitation is calculated by the ship's classification society.

Weather routing Service offered by a government department or private company whereby a shipowner or ship operator is provided with a route for his or her ship, devised by means of up-to-date weather predictions, which avoids severe weather conditions such as storms, fog and ice. This route is normally not the most direct but is expected to take less time as it avoids conditions that would require a reduction in speed. Additionally, the risks of heavy weather damage and, in extreme cases, of injury to the crew, are reduced. A fee is charged for this service. Also known as ship routing.

Weighbridge Plate on the ground onto which lorries can be driven in order to weigh them. The purpose of this is to determine whether the maximum permissible weight for a vehicle to be allowed on the roads has been exceeded. The use of a weighbridge also allows the weight of cargo to be ascertained by deducting the tare or weight of the vehicle (plus the shipping container, if any) from the gross weight. The weight obtained in this way is termed the **weighbridge weight**.

Weight cargo Cargo one tonne of which measures one cubic metre or less. Freight on a weight cargo is generally payable on the weight, that is, per tonne or per ton. Also referred to as deadweight cargo. *See Figs. 75, 126a, 143.*

Weight/measurement ratio Ratio of a cargo's weight to its cubic measurement, expressed in cubic feet to the ton or cubic metres to the tonne. This ratio can be used in conjunction with a ship's bale capacity or grain capacity, depending on the particular cargo, to determine the maximum quantity of cargo which can be loaded in a ship.

Well (1) Depression in a specially designed flatrack into which steel coils rest to prevent them from moving when in transit.

Well (2) Space between the forecastle and the bridge or between the poop and the bridge.

Wharf Structure built alongside the water where ships berth for loading or discharging goods. The person who owns or operates a wharf is known as a **wharfinger**. The charges payable by cargo interests for the use of a wharf are called **wharfage** or **wharfage charges**.

White products Refined products such as aviation spirit, motor spirit and kerosene. Also referred to as clean products or clean petroleum products.

Winch Piece of machinery consisting mainly of a revolving device, which is bolted to the deck of a ship. It has various uses: to raise and lower derrick ropes, to open and close hatches and to moor the ship.

Windage Quantity of cargo blown away by the wind during loading or discharging. This type of loss occurs to fine bulk cargoes.

Wine Liquid cargo widely carried in bulk in specialised ships known as **wine tankers**. These are handled at dedicated **wine terminals**, port terminals dedicated to the handling and storage of wine. Cargo is pumped out and conveyed in pipes between the quay and the tanks.

Wing Part of a ship located at the side of the hold. It is away from the square of the hatch and is therefore not accessible to cranes for loading, stowing and discharging. Cargo has to be moved into and out of the wings as a separate operation, often with the help of fork-lift trucks.

Wing tank Tank situated at the side of a ship such as a tanker, bulk carrier or combination carrier. The wing tank of a tanker extends the entire depth of the cargo space. One such tank is found on either side of a centre tank. These tanks are either the same size as the centre tank or smaller. The wing tank of a bulk carrier or combination carrier is most often located at the top of the hold and may be used for bulk cargoes, such as grain, or for water ballast.

Winter draught Depth of water to which a ship's hull may be immersed in a winter zone at certain times of the year. The depth is indicated by the winter load line painted on the ship's sides.

Winter freeboard Distance between the deck line of a ship and its winter load line.

Winter load line Line painted on the sides of a ship which shows the maximum depth to which that ship's hull may be immersed when in a winter zone. The line is painted with a W. Also referred to as **winter marks**.

Winter North Atlantic freeboard Distance between the deck line of a ship and its winter North Atlantic load line.

Winter North Atlantic load line Line painted on the sides of a ship, which shows the maximum depth to which that ship's hull may be immersed when in one of the North Atlantic winter seasonal zones. The line is marked WNA.

Winter North Atlantic timber freeboard

Winter North Atlantic timber freeboard   Distance between the deck line of a ship and its winter North Atlantic timber load line.

Winter North Atlantic timber load line   Line painted on the sides of a ship, which shows the maximum depth to which that ship's hull may be immersed when in one of the North Atlantic winter seasonal zones with a deck cargo of timber. The line is marked LWNA.

Winter timber freeboard   Distance between the deck line of a ship and its winter timber load line.

Winter timber load line   Line painted on the sides of a ship which shows the maximum depth to which the ship's hull may be immersed when in a winter zone with a deck cargo of timber. The line is marked LW.

Winter zone   One of the several geographical areas defined by the International Conference on Load Lines, where a ship's hull may be immersed no deeper than its winter load line at certain fixed times of the year.

Wire rod in coil   Thin gauge steel bars wound into coils of around one to two tonnes, widely transported worldwide and used to produce a variety of finished products. Coils are strapped in several places and care must be exercised when handling not to break the strapping. *See Figs.* **147a, 147b, 147c, 147d.**

Fig. 147a Wire rod in coil. In the illustrations, coils are being discharged from a ship onto the quay where they are lifted by fork-lift truck and placed onto an open area of ground to await onward transport by lorry

Figs. 147b, 147c and 147d Wire rod in coil. In the illustrations, coils are being discharged from a ship onto the quay where they are lifted by fork-lift truck and placed onto an open area of ground to await onward transport by lorry

Wire sling

Wire sling Strands of wire wound together into a rope and having a loop at each end for slinging round cargo and attaching to a crane for lifting. *See Fig. 148.*

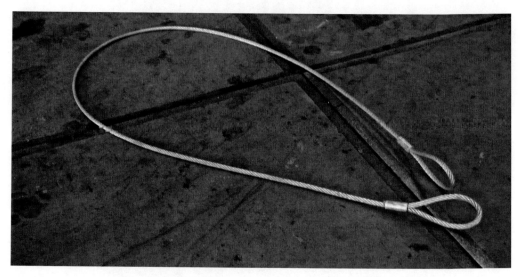

Fig. 148 Wire sling with a 1.5-tonne lifting capacity

Wood pellets Small uniform pieces of wood chippings used for fuel. They are accordingly a type of biomass. This type of cargo is carried in bulk carriers when in large quantities and loaded by spout into the holds. It is discharged by grab. It is carried in bulk containers when in smaller quantities. *See* **Biomass** *and* **Bulk container**.

Woodchips Small pieces of shredded timber of various types used in the paper-making industry. Woodchips are a type of biomass. Also spelled **wood chips**. *See* **Biomass, Woodchip carrier** *and* **Woodchip handling**.

Woodchip carrier Vessel designed to carry woodchips in bulk. Normally in the size range 20,000–60,000 tonnes deadweight, such vessels have a high cubic capacity because of the high stowage factor of this commodity which enables them to be loaded to their marks. Discharging is effected in one of various ways, for example by pneumatic conveyor belts or buckets. The advantage of woodchips over other timber products, as far as shipping them is concerned, is that they are quicker to handle and are consequently more economic to transport.

Woodchip handling Carried in woodchip carriers, woodchips are light and susceptible to being blown away during loading and discharging. The principal method of loading is by conveyor to a spout and of discharge by grab to a hopper, and thence often to a conveyor. Generally, nets surround the hopper to prevent chips blowing away and dust. *See Fig. 149*.

Fig. 149 Woodchips being transported in a barge

Woodpulp Product derived from wood by separating the fibres. It is used to make paper. It is shipped in large blocks or bales.

Woodpulp carrier Type of ship suitable for the carriage of woodpulp. The holds of the ship are box-shaped, that is, with vertical sides and having no obstructions, so as to allow the cargo, which is presented in large blocks, to be stowed efficiently. Some ships have side doors to allow loading of these blocks of woodpulp when they are palletised. If the ship is used to carry paper reels, it must have adequate dehumidifying equipment.

Yacht carrier Vessel capable of transporting yachts. Such ships may be purpose-built or may carry other cargoes as well. Yachts are carried under deck and on deck. They are secured upright in cradles.